20 Questions®

Warning: Small parts may be a choking hazard. Not for children under 3 years.

ACKNOWLEDGEMENTS

Editorial Director: Erin Conley
Designer: Jeanette Miller
Special thanks to Suzanne Cracraft, Emily Jocson, Scott Mednick, Jeff Pinsker,
Scott Setrakian and Lani Stackel for their invaluable assistance and contributions!

Spinner Books, a division of

University Games Corporation
2030 Harrison Street San Francisco, CA 94110

University Games Europe B.V.,
Australiëlaan 52, 6199 AA Maastricht Airport, Netherlands.

University Games Australia,
10 Apollo Street, Warriewood, Australia 2102.

Library of Congress-in-Publication Data on file with the publisher

ISBN 1-57528-916-4

Printed in China

04 05 MP 9 8 7 6 5 4 3

CONTENTS

RULES

For 1 or more players!

OBJECT
The object of the game is to show off your smarts by correctly identifying 10 well-known mystery topics through a series of clues.

STARTING THE GAME
The youngest player spins the spinner and says, "I am a _____ (Person, Place, Thing or Year)" as shown on the spinner. The youngest player then becomes that Person, Place, Thing or Year for this round of play. This player acts solely as a reader and may not guess until someone answers correctly.

GETTING A CLUE
The Reader must now flip to the start of the determined category (i.e. Person, Place, Thing or Year) and read clue number one aloud to the group.

After listening to the clue, the player to the Reader's left (a.k.a. the Guesser) has 10 seconds to guess who (or what) the Reader is. (Players may only guess when it's their turn.)

If the Guesser guesses correctly, s/he scores one point. The player to the Reader's right becomes the new Reader and starts with the next topic in the same category.

If the Guesser guesses incorrectly, the player to his/her left gets the next clue and may then try to crack the 20 Questions mystery.

Once all players have acted as the Reader, it is time to spin again! The player to the left of the last person to spin now spins to determine the type of category to be played. S/he is the first Reader for this round. If the same category has already been spun, continue where you left off.

Tip: Even if your guess sounds silly, just say it. There is no penalty for an incorrect guess! And statistics show that you have no chance of winning if you don't make a guess.

WINNING THE GAME
The first player to score 10 points wins the game!

PLAYING ON YOUR OWN
You get to be the Reader *and* the Guesser! Keep track of how many clues it takes to guess the correct answer. Get eight topics correct in less than 40 clues and you're a winner!

INTRO

Remember playing **20 Questions** as a kid? Throughout my childhood I recall my father frequently enlivening our dinner conversation with a modified version of the game. "Are you an animal, vegetable, or mineral?" he would ask. My sister and I would race to come up with our mystery topic. His challenge was to guess our identity in less than 20 questions. Our challenge was to answer his questions accurately. He would often stump us with questions like, "Do you prefer guns to butter?" or "Do you live in Europe?" We always had lots of fun—and always learned something new.

I was thrilled when University Games introduced the board game **20 Questions** after designer Scott Mednick and I met at a friend's 30th birthday. Scott suggested collaborating and I jumped at the chance to work with him. The results were more than seven different games, translated into eight languages, and more than two million games in homes worldwide. Now the book!

Spinner Books are a great way to combine a game and a book. Each one can be read and enjoyed alone or played with a group of friends and family. I hope that you share this book and get a taste of the fun, laughter and spirited rivalry that filled my family's dining room in Clayton, Missouri.

Have fun reading and playing!

Bob

PEOPLE

2O Questions®

INSTRUCT PLAYERS THAT "I AM A PERSON."

1 I went from a successful movie career to an equally successful TV career.

2 I first achieved fame in 1935 in a series of short films.

3 I have four legs, but walk on two.

4 I'm not too smart.

5 I'm plump.

6 I'm an expert on Bugs, but I'm not an entomologist.

7 I am an animal.

8 Lookout! I wear shirts, but no pants.

9 My girlfriend is Petunia.

10 I have straight hair and a curly tail.

11 I'm p-p-p-p-p-porcine.

12 I am a cartoon character.

13 My stutter is often imitated.

14 I don't like to be called "the other white meat."

15 I end a lot of Warner Brothers cartoons.

16 My first and last names start with the same letter.

17 You won't find me in a sty.

18 My goodbye is "That's All Folks!"

19 I know Elmer Fudd and Yosemite Sam.

20 I don't eat that much, but I've been called a pig.

I am Porky Pig.

2O Questions

INSTRUCT PLAYERS THAT "I AM A PERSON."

1 I am a living American female.

2 I was born in 1967.

3 I am best known as an actress.

4 I'm 5'9" tall.

5 *People* magazine has called me one of America's sexiest people.

6 I turned down Gwyneth Paltrow's Oscar®-winning role in *Shakespeare in Love*.

7 My brother is an actor.

8 I was born in the South.

9 *Entertainment Weekly* listed me as one of the 25 greatest actresses of the 1990s.

10 I won the Golden Globe for Best Actress in 2001.

11 I graduated from Georgia's Campbell High School in 1985.

12 In 1989, I ate a *Mystic Pizza*.

13 I have costarred with Mel Gibson, Hugh Grant and Brad Pitt.

14 You might have seen me in *Steel Magnolias*.

15 I married a country music star.

16 *Forbes* named me the "most powerful celebrity on the planet" in 2000.

17 Richard Gere and I reunited on-screen in 1999.

18 In *My Best Friend's Wedding* I tried to steal the groom.

19 I've played a runaway bride and I've been one.

20 I've been called a pretty woman and I've played one.

I am Julia Roberts.

2O Questions

INSTRUCT PLAYERS THAT "I AM A PERSON."

1 I was born in Illinois.

2 I had four wives.

3 I was an avid fisherman.

4 I vacationed along Lake Charlesvoix.

5 You can call me Papa.

6 I won the Nobel Prize for Literature.

7 One of my novels was published posthumously in 1986.

8 I slept with the light on.

9 I loved a good bullfight.

10 I had nearly fifty cats—their descendents still roam my historic home.

11 My "sunrise" effort as a serious novelist came in 1926.

12 I found myself in the Lost Generation.

13 I drove an ambulance in World War I.

14 Two of my granddaughters are famous.

15 I committed suicide in 1961.

16 When I was there, Paris was *A Moveable Feast*.

17 When I'm being Ernest, I'm being myself.

18 I wrote about an old man and the sea.

19 I challenged Senator Joseph McCarthy to a boxing match.

20 I've been known to hang out at Harry's Bar.

I am Ernest Hemingway.

2O Questions

INSTRUCT PLAYERS THAT "I AM A PERSON."

1 I was born in Duluth, Minnesota.

2 I am a living American male.

3 Although I'm Jewish, I found Jesus.

4 I named myself after a poet.

5 I am a musician.

6 I have won Grammy Awards.

7 I star in a Sam Peckinpah film.

8 I play the harmonica and the guitar.

9 I was a social figure in the 1960s.

10 I sang to feed starving people in Bangladesh.

11 I toured with The Grateful Dead.

12 My real name is Zimmerman.

13 I was featured in D. A. Pennebaker's film *Don't Look Back*.

14 I am a Travelling Wilbury.

15 Sometimes it's hard to understand what I'm singing.

16 I sang about a black tap dancer.

17 My son Jakob is a Wallflower.

18 I revisited Highway 61 in the 1960s.

19 I said, "The times they are a changin'."

20 I asked, "How many roads must a man walk down?"

I am Bob Dylan.

2O Questions

INSTRUCT PLAYERS THAT "I AM A PERSON."

1 I am a female.
2 I was a queen at 17.
3 I am said to have committed suicide.
4 I am the subject of a play by George Bernard Shaw.
5 Shakespeare wrote about me.
6 People describe me as a woman floating down "denial river."
7 I was born in 69 B.C.
8 My first two husbands were my younger brothers.
9 I ruled Egypt, but my family was actually Macedonian.
10 Elizabeth Taylor put on some heavy eye makeup to portray me.
11 I made my Marc over 2,000 years ago.
12 In 1934, Cecil B. DeMille produced a film about me.
13 I was Egypt's last ruler before the Romans.
14 My needle doesn't help much in sewing.
15 I was part of a world famous love story.
16 I used cosmetics 2,000 years before Helena Rubenstein did.
17 I walked like an Egyptian.
18 I lived in Alexandria.
19 I belong to the Ptolemaic Dynasty.
20 Julius Caesar was the father of my first child.

I am Cleopatra.

2O Questions

INSTRUCT PLAYERS THAT "I AM A PERSON."

1 My brother played professional baseball.
2 I was born in the same year World War I began.
3 I am an American male.
4 I played the field.
5 I was a hit man.
6 I was nicknamed after a ship.
7 I wore pinstripes to work.
8 I loved making coffee.
9 My career began in San Francisco.
10 I started work in 1932.
11 I was a Yankee, but I spent time in the South.
12 I retired in 1951.
13 I am in the Hall of Fame.
14 1939 was a streaky year for me.
15 I hit over 360 homers.
16 Simon and Garfunkel looked for me in the late 1960s.
17 I was born in Martinez, California.
18 I died in 1999.
19 I was married to America's most beloved blonde.
20 My parents spoke Italian.

I am Joe DiMaggio.

2❂ Que$ti❂n$

INSTRUCT PLAYERS THAT "I AM A PERSON."

1 I am known for my smile.

2 I am male.

3 I graduated from the U.S. Naval Academy.

4 I'm a Democrat.

5 Inflation deflated me.

6 My middle name is Earl.

7 I married Rosalynn Smith.

8 I ran my family's peanut business.

9 I helped mediate Israeli-Egyptian peace negotiations.

10 I was deeply affected by the Iranian hostage crisis.

11 I slept in the White House.

12 I ran with Fritz.

13 My mom, Lillian, and younger brother, Billy, got more attention than I did.

14 I sold the presidential yacht.

15 I was governor of Georgia in the 1970s.

16 I passed significant environmental legislation.

17 Jody Powell handled my press.

18 I wrote *An Hour Before Daylight*.

19 My youngest child is named Amy.

20 I became the 39th president of the United States.

I am Jimmy Carter.

2O QUESTIONS®

INSTRUCT PLAYERS THAT "I AM A PERSON."

1 I was born in Michigan in 1950.
2 The Rolling Stones opened for me in the 1960s. I opened for them in the 1970s.
3 I've won more than 15 Grammies.
4 I am an American male.
5 I first appeared in the credits of a 1964 Frankie Avalon movie.
6 My career began at age 12.
7 Some people say I'm a musical genius.
8 I'm not "Little" anymore.
9 I did an entire soundtrack for a Spike Lee film.
10 One of my hits is a tribute to Duke Ellington.
11 Motown Records signed, sealed and delivered me.
12 I play the harmonica and twelve other instruments.
13 I wear sunglasses, even at night.
14 I'm pretty mellow but I had a pop hit with "Uptight."
15 My name sounds like a kind of bread.
16 For decades, my record sales have been "Hotter than July."
17 When I got older, I decided to start wearing my hair in braids.
18 You can see me, but I can't see you.
19 My name at birth was Steveland Morris.
20 My early hit was "Fingertips, Part 2."

I am Stevie Wonder.

2O QUESTIONS

INSTRUCT PLAYERS THAT "I AM A PERSON."

1 I am in the movies.

2 My sister was murdered.

3 I wore black before it was fashionable.

4 My alter ego is named Miss Gulch.

5 I can fly.

6 I can cast a spell.

7 Margaret Hamilton played me in the movies.

8 People dress up like me on Halloween.

9 L. Frank Baum wrote books about me.

10 Winged monkeys do my bidding.

11 I like to frighten everyone.

12 There are three W's in my name.

13 Water makes me melt.

14 My broom does more than sweep.

15 I'm green.

16 If I was good, my name might be Glenda.

17 Dorothy stole my broom.

18 I am the author of *Surrender, Dorothy*.

19 To me, East is least and West is best.

20 I live near the Land of Oz.

I am the Wicked Witch of the West.

2O QUESTIONS

INSTRUCT PLAYERS THAT "I AM A PERSON."

1 I am a living American female.

2 I am a 20th century artist.

3 I hang out in Hollywood, but I'm not an actor.

4 In 1975 I toured with The Rolling Stones.

5 My name is more recognizable than my face.

6 I've covered *Time* magazine, but I'm not a reporter.

7 I shot the last portrait of John Lennon before his tragic death in 1980.

8 My work covers modern American newsmakers.

9 I was born in Connecticut in 1947.

10 If I shoot you, you won't bleed.

11 To me, the world is often just black and white.

12 My initials are A. L., but I'm not Amy Lesser.

13 I have to wait to see how things develop before finishing a day's work.

14 I bring a camera or two to work.

15 Richard Avedon is one of my colleagues.

16 I graduated from the San Francisco Art Institute in 1971.

17 I'm the first woman to exhibit her photographic work in the Smithsonian Institution.

18 My book *Women* was released in 2000.

19 I work with stars, but I'm not an astronomer.

20 I share my first name with a little orphan.

I am Annie Leibovitz.

2O Questions

INSTRUCT PLAYERS THAT "I AM A PERSON."

1   I am a political leader.
2   I'm a pretty nice guy, but the British government was scared of me.
3   I am male.
4   My great goal was realized in 1947.
5   I exemplify the moral life.
6   A 1980s movie told my story.
7   I am a vegetarian.
8   Dr. Martin Luther King, Jr. followed my teachings.
9   I agitated for national independence.
10   I instituted a hand spinning and weaving program.
11   My kind of fast doesn't involve speed.
12   I was assassinated in 1948.
13   I believe that freedom cannot be taken by force.
14   I studied law in London.
15   I am a spiritual leader.
16   My first name is Mohandas.
17   I believe in non-violent civil disobedience.
18   I lived in South Africa, then returned home.
19   Ben Kingsley played me in the movies.
20   I was jailed and jailed again.

I am Gandhi.

2O Questions

INSTRUCT PLAYERS THAT "I AM A PERSON."

1 I became a legend in my own time.

2 I was criticized for the good I did.

3 I was a pioneer in my field.

4 I became a national heroine.

5 I was born in 1820.

6 I influenced generations of women.

7 I grew up in England.

8 I was the force behind the enactment of the Contagious Disease Act.

9 I am a woman.

10 I was an early feminist.

11 I ministered during the Crimean War.

12 I established a training school for midwives.

13 I organized the Sanitary Commission of India office.

14 I was a reformer of hospitals.

15 Lord Houghton was in love with me.

16 I share my first name with a city in Italy.

17 I initiated the modern era of nursing.

18 My last name sounds like a singing bird.

19 I was called the "Lady with the Lamp."

20 My initials are F. N.

I am Florence Nightingale.

2O Questions

INSTRUCT PLAYERS THAT "I AM A PERSON."

1. I was born in Philadelphia.
2. My father was a guitarist.
3. My career, and my life, had its ups and downs.
4. I'm known as one of the greatest singers of the 20th century.
5. I am an African American.
6. People know I sing the blues.
7. Diana Ross plays me in the movies.
8. My first name is usually a boy's.
9. I am a lady.
10. New York was my kind of town in the 1940s.
11. Ken Burns featured me in his TV series *Jazz*.
12. I've asked for a pig foot and a bottle of beer.
13. I've looked into "Them There Eyes."
14. I count Count Basie among my collaborators.
15. Some call me Lady Day.
16. I was a heavy drinker and drug abuser.
17. I say, "God Bless the Child . . . "
18. My first name is not William.
19. Some say I ruined my voice.
20. My last name sounds like a day off.

I am Billie Holliday.

2⊙ Questions

INSTRUCT PLAYERS THAT "I AM A PERSON."

1 I am a living American woman.

2 I was born in 1957.

3 Dustin Hoffman checked me out in *Tootsie*.

4 I became a model after graduating from Boston University.

5 In 1991, I drove off a cliff with Louise.

6 I was raised in New England.

7 I am over six feet tall.

8 I am considered very smart, by Hollywood standards.

9 I played the mother of a little mouse in 1999.

10 I won a Best Actress in a Supporting Role Oscar® for playing a dog trainer.

11 My hair is usually auburn.

12 I have costarred with Michael Keaton, Susan Sarandon and Madonna.

13 It took a fly to make me famous.

14 I tried out for the U.S. Olympic archery team in 2000.

15 I've headed down the aisle three times.

16 I made a famous fashion faux pas at the 1992 Oscars®.

17 I share my name with Ozzie and Sammy.

18 When I played professional baseball onscreen, I was a catcher.

19 My TV show debuted in 2000 and had a short-lived run.

20 I am best known as an actress.

I am Geena Davis.

2O Questions

INSTRUCT PLAYERS THAT "I AM A PERSON."

1 I live under the name of Sanders.

2 My Robin doesn't have a red breast.

3 I am British.

4 There's a house at my corner.

5 I'm known for being stout, not smart.

6 I've been scared of my own tracks.

7 I love to eat, but I'm always stuffed.

8 I show up in stories that a father told to his son.

9 It all started *When We Were Very Young*.

10 My real name is Edward Bear.

11 My story was first published in 1926.

12 I'm not scary but my last name rhymes with "boo."

13 I live in the Hundred Acre Wood.

14 My friends include a donkey, a rabbit, a tiger, a pig and a boy.

15 My last name makes children giggle.

16 My middle name is "the."

17 I've braved bees and trees for honey.

18 I am animated by Disney.

19 Ernest H. Shepard drew me.

20 I hope that people will bear with me.

I am Winnie the Pooh.

2O QuesτɪⓄNs

INSTRUCT PLAYERS THAT "I AM A PERSON."

1 I am a living American male.
2 I am an actor.
3 I was born in Oklahoma in 1963.
4 I was raised in the Show Me State.
5 I worked as the El Pollo Loco chicken before becoming an actor.
6 I'm not related to Pittsburgh's founder.
7 I have blond hair and blue eyes.
8 I attended the University of Missouri.
9 Christian Slater interviewed me regarding my nocturnal eating habits.
10 In 1992, Robert Redford took me fishing.
11 I've been to *Kalifornia*.
12 Actress Juliette Lewis was a long time steady of mine.
13 My B. P. doesn't stand for British Petroleum.
14 *People* magazine named me the "Sexiest Man Alive."
15 I hitched a ride from Thelma and Louise.
16 I got famous in *The Legends of the Fall*.
17 I dated Gwyneth Paltrow.
18 In 2000, I married a television star.
19 I went to Mexico with Julia Roberts in 2001.
20 Guy Ritchie directed me in *Snatch*.

I am Brad Pitt.

2O Questions

INSTRUCT PLAYERS THAT "I AM A PERSON."

1 I am male.

2 My middle name is Elias.

3 I was born in Chicago.

4 I am a motion picture producer.

5 I set up my first studio in a garage.

6 My studio has won more than 50 Academy Awards®.

7 My name is a household word.

8 *Steamboat Willie* was my first success.

9 I am a huge Annette Funicello fan.

10 I died in 1966.

11 In one of my greatest artistic achievements, The Philadelphia Symphony Orchestra plays backup to my wizard.

12 I put a duck in a sailor suit.

13 I had my own club but wasn't a member.

14 I knew Mortimer before Mickey.

15 I have my own land and my own world.

16 My TV series made Davy Crockett an idol in the 1950s.

17 My cartoon *Flowers and Trees* was the first film in full Technicolor.

18 When I started my own business in 1923, people thought I was goofy.

19 From Minnie to Mulan, I've had some glamorous gals working for my company.

20 I made the first full-length animated film.

I am Walt Disney.

2O QUESTIONS

INSTRUCT PLAYERS THAT "I AM A PERSON."

1 I was born in Fairfield, Connecticut on November 19, 1961.
2 I am a living American.
3 I am female.
4 I am best known as an actress.
5 I have blond hair and blue eyes.
6 My film debut was in 1981's *Rich and Famous*.
7 In the 1980s I was a regular member of the daytime soap *As the World Turns*.
8 I won the Golden Globe for Best Actress in 1990 and 1994.
9 I have co-starred with Mel Gibson, Nicholas Cage, Val Kilmer and Billy Crystal.
10 I lived in San Francisco in the 1980s.
11 Tom Hanks once got me to climb a volcano.
12 In 1994, I won the Harvard Hasty Pudding Award for "Woman of the Year."
13 In 1991, I played Jim Morrison's wife in *The Doors*.
14 When I met Harry I was Sally.
15 You might have seen me as Goose's wife in *Top Gun*.
16 When I'm in New York, I go to the top of the Empire State Building.
17 I married—and divorced—Dennis Quaid.
18 My fake orgasm scene is a classic movie moment.
19 My real name is Margaret.
20 In *I.Q.*, I wasn't as smart as Walter Matthau's Einstein.

I am Meg Ryan.

2O QueStiONS

INSTRUCT PLAYERS THAT "I AM A PERSON."

1 I am American.
2 I made art my day job.
3 I died in 1987.
4 I am male.
5 I've got my own museum in Pittsburgh, Pennsylvania.
6 My early career was in commercial illustration.
7 I am a filmmaker.
8 You can see my work at the Metropolitan Museum of Art.
9 I have no children, but I am called pop.
10 I managed Lou Reed when he was "underground."
11 Dollar bills and Jacqueline Kennedy mean the same to me.
12 To me, Marilyn Monroe was just another can of soup.
13 I produced silk screen paintings.
14 Contrary to a certain movie title, I was never shot.
15 I did a film satire on Frankenstein.
16 I wrote two autobiographies.
17 I founded the magazine *Interview*.
18 Fifteen minutes became a lifetime for me.
19 I wore glasses.
20 I made Campbell's® soup a work of art.

I am Andy Warhol.

2◉ Questi◉ns

20

INSTRUCT PLAYERS THAT "I AM A PERSON."

1 I am a scholar, an athlete, a musician and a politician.

2 I have been called a "moral censor."

3 I am among history's greatest thinkers.

4 I was born in 551 B.C.

5 I believe in man's duty to man.

6 I am a teacher.

7 I influenced 2,000 years of Eastern thought.

8 I am Chinese.

9 Over 370 million people follow my words closely.

10 To some I sound like a riddle.

11 My words offer guides for living.

12 I am a writer.

13 I influence an entire culture.

14 My name is not confusing.

15 Fortune cookies spread my word.

16 People made sacrifices to me for centuries after my death.

17 I am a male.

18 My favorite game is Mah-Jong.

19 People are always quoting me.

20 Add "ism" to my name and you've got a religion.

I am Confucius.

20 Questions

INSTRUCT PLAYERS THAT "I AM A PERSON."

1 I am a dead American male.

2 I was born in 1835.

3 I was born in Florida, Missouri.

4 I wrote 28 books and lots of short stories.

5 I never let my schooling interfere with my education.

6 My real middle name is Langhorne.

7 I called a classic "a book that people praise, but don't read."

8 Hemingway said that all American literature comes from one of my books.

9 At 17, I became a river pilot's apprentice.

10 I created a famous Finn who never visited Finland.

11 My Hannibal is not a cannibal.

12 My pen name was inspired by some river terminology.

13 My river is the Mississippi.

14 My father was a judge.

15 I've seen frogs jump.

16 People flip for my Wilson.

17 I've created princes and paupers.

18 I sent a Yankee to see King Arthur.

19 I spent a cold summer in San Francisco.

20 My real first name is Samuel.

I am Mark Twain.

2O Questions

INSTRUCT PLAYERS THAT "I AM A PERSON."

1 America first saw me in the 1960s.
2 I have one daughter and no sons.
3 I am a fictional character.
4 My job is the pits.
5 Bowling is my favorite sport.
6 I'm a member of the Water Buffalo Lodge.
7 My world is full of historical anachronisms.
8 My car doesn't use gas.
9 My fences are made of stone.
10 Everyone I know wears animal fur.
11 I started on prime-time TV.
12 William Hanna and Joseph Barbera created me.
13 Alan Reed is my voice.
14 Mr. Slate is my boss.
15 My daughter wears a bone in her hair.
16 Some compare the wife and me to Ralph and Alice Kramden.
17 I have my own vitamins and cereal.
18 Brontosaurus burgers are my favorite food.
19 My first name and last name start with the same letter.
20 John Goodman played me in the movies.

I am Fred Flintstone.

2O Questıons

INSTRUCT PLAYERS THAT "I AM A PERSON."

1. I made four movies.
2. I started in 1959.
3. I am in the Rock and Roll Hall of Fame.
4. I introduced the Blue Meanies to the world.
5. I am a group of four.
6. I am British.
7. One of my works is all white.
8. My last live concert was in San Francisco.
9. My company sued Apple Computer.
10. In 2000, an anthology about me topped the bestseller list.
11. Stu was the first to leave me.
12. My British invasion wasn't in 1812.
13. I broke up in 1970.
14. I may be Liverpool's most famous export.
15. Part of me married a Japanese artist.
16. My hairdo was the moptop.
17. Although Pete was Best, I did better without him.
18. My John and Paul have nothing to do with the Vatican.
19. I hate to brag, but I pretty much define the 1960s.
20. *The Ed Sullivan Show* introduced me to America.

I am The Beatles.

2O Questions

INSTRUCT PLAYERS THAT "I AM A PERSON."

1 I am male.
2 I was born in 1962.
3 I dropped out of high school to pursue my dream.
4 I got my start at Yuk Yuk Comedy Club in Toronto.
5 My first TV series was the *Duck Factory* in 1983.
6 I played an extra-terrestrial in *Earth Girls are Easy*.
7 I'm one of the highest-paid actors in Hollywood.
8 I've been called a joker, but I played a Riddler.
9 I was cast as the "token white guy" on *In Living Color*.
10 I've been called a liar.
11 My second wife played a police officer on *Picket Fences*.
12 REM sang the theme song to my 1999 biographical film.
13 I have co-starred with Jeff Daniels, Jeff Goldblum and Danny Devito.
14 My physical comedy reminds some of Jerry Lewis.
15 People aren't sure if I am dumb, dumber or dumbest.
16 I dated Nurse Betty in 2000.
17 I like Christmas, but in 2000 I was a real Grinch.
18 I starred as me and myself in a 2000 Farrelly Brothers film.
19 I was America's first pet detective.
20 Some think I'm a comedic genius.

I am Jim Carrey.

2O Questions

INSTRUCT PLAYERS THAT "I AM A PERSON."

1 My favorite number is less than 50.

2 I dress in uniforms to go to work.

3 I can usually do a lot in two minutes.

4 I won it all back to back.

5 I have won at least five Superbowls.

6 I am a sports team.

7 Peter Harris became my president and CEO in 2000.

8 The 1980s were my best decade.

9 I am in the NFL.

10 One of my stars was Tittle-ating.

11 My legendary stars include Frankie Albert.

12 My faithful follow mc on Sundays.

13 If you know "The Catch," you know me.

14 My city shows up in my name.

15 My colors are red and gold.

16 The gold rush inspired my name.

17 I moved Montana from Indiana to California.

18 I was the first professional sports franchise on the West Coast.

19 I'm not much into Rams or Falcons.

20 My mascot is Sourdough Sam.

I am the San Francisco 49ers.

20 Questions

INSTRUCT PLAYERS THAT "I AM A PERSON."

1 I have a British accent.

2 I believe in experiencing art.

3 I am female.

4 P. L. Travers wrote a series of books about me.

5 Jane and Michael are my charges.

6 I am fictional.

7 I am known to pop in and pop out.

8 My film won five Academy Awards® in 1964, including Best Actress and Best Song.

9 I worked for the Banks, but I know nothing of investments.

10 My carpetbag is much bigger than it looks.

11 I worked at Number 17 Cherry Tree Lane.

12 I tend to leave when the wind changes.

13 I enjoy flying kites.

14 Walt Disney made a film about me.

15 I advocate taking medication with sugar.

16 Some have called me "Nanny."

17 I have a good friend who is a chimney sweep.

18 I always travel with an umbrella.

19 Julie Andrews played me in a movie.

20 Supercalifragilisticexpialidocious!

I am Mary Poppins.

2⊙ Questi⊚ns

INSTRUCT PLAYERS THAT "I AM A PERSON."

1 I play the clarinet.

2 I am male.

3 I was born in 1935.

4 I wear glasses.

5 I appeared in the James Bond film *Casino Royale*.

6 I can write, act and direct.

7 *Play It Again, Sam* was my take on Bogart's *Casablanca*.

8 I share my first name with an old car.

9 Some might call me neurotic.

10 I wrote a humorous book, *Without Feathers*.

11 I named my son after Satchel Page.

12 I interviewed Zelig.

13 My real name is Allen Stewart Konigsberg.

14 I am Jewish.

15 In some circles, I'm known for my *Crimes and Misdemeanors*.

16 Manhattan is home to me.

17 In *Annie Hall*, I gave Sigourney Weaver her start.

18 Mia Farrow and Diane Keaton starred in many of my films.

19 I won an Academy Award® for Best Director in 1977.

20 I married my lover's adopted daughter.

I am Woody Allen.

2O QUESTIONS

INSTRUCT PLAYERS THAT "I AM A PERSON."

1 I was born in 1954.
2 My Harpo is not a Marx.
3 I anchored the *AM Chicago Show*.
4 I have worked as a news reporter.
5 I am from Koscuisko, Mississippi.
6 I am female.
7 Like Madonna, I'm known by my distinctive first name.
8 My favorite poet is Maya Angelou.
9 I was an abused child.
10 Some say I caused Phil to spill.
11 My primetime is during the day, not the night.
12 I'll never let you forget your spirit.
13 I was in the film *Native Son*.
14 I helped launch a new TV network in 2000.
15 I have a live audience at work.
16 My best friend is named Gail.
17 I appear in the film *The Color Purple*.
18 *The National Enquirer* keeps tabs on my weight.
19 My book club can really sell books.
20 I host a TV show that bears my name.

I am Oprah Winfrey.

PLACES

2O Questions®

INSTRUCT PLAYERS THAT "I AM A PLACE."

1 Six nations have flown their flags over me.
2 I am in America.
3 I was the 28th to join my union.
4 I like Ike. He's one of my native sons.
5 I have a panhandle.
6 My toast has nothing to do with drinking.
7 I house NASA's Johnson Space Center.
8 My largest city is named for Sam.
9 I border Mexico.
10 Most people prefer red, but my favorite rose is yellow.
11 I was biggest until Alaska.
12 Although I only have one star, I'm not really alone.
13 I'm a five-letter state.
14 Don't mess with me.
15 My baseball team is named for law enforcement officers.
16 Everything is bigger in me.
17 People sing about being deep in my heart.
18 I still remember the Alamo.
19 I'm not greasy, but I boast a quarter of the U.S.'s oil.
20 George W. Bush calls me home.

I am Texas.

2O Questions

INSTRUCT PLAYERS THAT "I AM A PLACE."

1 I produce the world's largest crops of hazelnuts and raisins.

2 My currency is the lira.

3 Ninety-nine percent of my citizens are Islamic.

4 I share my name with something quite fowl.

5 My Republic was founded in 1923.

6 Mustafa Kemal Pasha is my father.

7 I form a bridge between two continents.

8 Visit me and try borek and dolma.

9 I have been inhabited since 6,500 B.C.

10 I don't know Helen, but I know Troy.

11 I am a European, Mediterranean and Middle Eastern country.

12 Istanbul is my largest city.

13 I am home to the Grand Bazaar.

14 Ephesus and Cappadocia are my ancient sites.

15 I border Bulgaria.

16 Whirling dervishes originated with me.

17 I am known for carpets and coffee.

18 I am home to the Blue Mosque.

19 The Bosphorus Strait divides my country.

20 My capital is Ankara.

I am Turkey.

2O Questions®

INSTRUCT PLAYERS THAT "I AM A PLACE."

1 My population is 3.5 million people.
2 My north is warmer than my south.
3 Abel Tasman first saw me.
4 I am part of the Commonwealth.
5 My national symbol is a nocturnal bird.
6 I call an undershirt a singlet and a washcloth a flannel.
7 I celebrate the signing of the treaty of Waitangi on February 14.
8 I have three main islands.
9 I farm perna canaliculas at my Marlborough Sound.
10 Rugby is my favorite sport.
11 My people drink Lion and Steinlager.
12 Eighty million sheep inhabit my land.
13 I won the last America's Cup of the 20th century.
14 The first man to climb Mt. Everest came from here.
15 My accent sounds British but I'm not from Britain.
16 The Maori are my native people.
17 My highest mountain is Mt. Cook.
18 My capital is Wellington.
19 I'm known for my Kiwis.
20 Many incorrectly associate me with Australia.

I am New Zealand.

2O Questions

INSTRUCT PLAYERS THAT "I AM A PLACE."

1 When people visit me, I take their breath away.

2 Jon Krakauer wrote about me.

0 Yes sir, I was named for a George.

4 I always feel like I'm on top of the world.

5 I was formed about 60 million years ago.

6 I'm always feeling high.

7 I'm always cold.

8 Come see me if someone tells you to take a hike.

9 Avalanches have caused most of my fatalities.

10 I'm covered with snow.

11 I'm on the border of Tibet.

12 Sir Edmund Hillary is best known for climbing all over me.

13 I'm located in the Himalayas.

14 In 1999, I was found to be six feet higher than previously thought.

15 The Khumbu Ice Fall is my most dangerous area.

16 I'm not a cemetery, but there are approximately 120 corpses on my grounds.

17 Sherpas know me best.

18 In Nepal, I'm called "The Goddess of the Sky."

19 I'm the highest of my kind in the world.

20 My English name derives from the first person that recorded my height and location.

I am Mt. Everest.

2O Questions

INSTRUCT PLAYERS THAT "I AM A PLACE."

1 My hills are the greenest green.
2 I was finally settled in 1851.
3 I am American.
4 I am in the western half of the U.S.
5 I hosted the 1962 World's Fair.
6 I see rain over half the time.
7 I am home to Smith Tower.
8 I held the first U.S. labor strike.
9 I am home to Boeing.
10 I have Huskies, but I'm not Alaska.
11 I offer ferry service to a foreign country.
12 I am in the Evergreen State.
13 I am the largest city in my region.
14 The richest man in the world calls me home.
15 My needle won't fit in a sewing box.
16 Fraiser calls me home.
17 I was the gateway to Alaska's gold rush.
18 My Pilots left, but my Mariners stayed.
19 Amazon.com calls me home.
20 My local brew is Ranier Beer.

I am Seattle, Washington.

2O Questions®

INSTRUCT PLAYERS THAT "I AM A PLACE."

1. I am north of the equator.
2. I am a country.
3. I have my own alphabet.
4. I am in Asia.
5. My people are Buddhists.
6. I have elephants.
7. My food is hot and spicy.
8. Singha is my favorite beer.
9. Despite my name, I'm not known for my ties.
10. I am known as "The Land of Smiles."
11. I'm the only Southeast Asian country never ruled by Europeans.
12. My Patpong Road is a male tourist mecca.
13. Phuket, Pei Pei and Koh Samui are my islands.
14. You might ride a tuk tuk here.
15. Visit me and see the bridge over the River Kwai.
16. I am home to the Golden Triangle.
17. My sapphires and silk are famous.
18. I border Myanmar, Laos and Cambodia.
19. Anna visited my former king.
20. My capital is Bangkok.

I am Thailand.

2O Questions

INSTRUCT PLAYERS THAT "I AM A PLACE."

1 I have a river that flows backward.

2 I am the 21st of my kind.

3 I am in America.

4 I am a leading agricultural state.

5 I am part of the Corn Belt.

6 The last letter of my name is silent.

7 Enrico Fermi conducted the first nuclear reaction in my land.

8 My name comes from the Native American word for "superior men."

9 Kaskaskia Island is my only part west of the Mississippi River.

10 Louis Sullivan and Frank Lloyd Wright gave me much of my look.

11 I am the Land of Lincoln.

12 I am the Prairie State.

13 I am home to Peoria.

14 I have three Is and no mouth.

15 I am Ronald Reagan's home state.

16 Indiana, Kentucky and Iowa are my neighbors.

17 Tornadoes are a big killer of mine.

18 The *ER* is in my state.

19 Al Capone's illegal liquor ring was based in my largest city.

20 I've got the "Windy City."

I am Illinois.

2O Questions®

INSTRUCT PLAYERS THAT "I AM A PLACE."

1 I am in the Atlantic Ocean.
2 My name is shapely.
3 My Keys don't open locks.
4 I extend from Miami, Florida to San Juan, Puerto Rico.
5 I am a mystery.
6 Wonder Woman's home is within my boundaries.
7 I am not recognized by the U.S. Board of Geographic Names.
8 I am imaginary.
9 I'm not a Monkee, but I know Davey Jones.
10 I touch the U.S.
11 I am part of the Caribbean.
12 In me, a compass points true north.
13 The Japanese call me the Devil's Sea.
14 My Gulf Stream is extremely swift and turbulent.
15 My weather patterns are very unpredictable.
16 *Argosy* had me on its cover in August 1968.
17 It is believed that I have taken down ships and planes.
18 My first name is also an island.
19 I sound like I might be equilateral.
20 My favorite shape has three points.

I am the Bermuda Triangle.

2O QUESTIONS

INSTRUCT PLAYERS THAT "I AM A PLACE."

1 I'm American.

2 The Mississippi River runs east of me.

3 I am home to an active volcano.

4 I am the largest city in my state.

5 I get more than 29 million visitors a year.

6 I am in the desert.

7 My state is the Silver State.

8 The Hoover Dam is in my neighborhood.

9 Bugsy Siegel got me started.

10 My airport is McCarran International Airport.

11 I am famous for my buffets.

12 My downtown is Glitter Gulch.

13 I call myself the Entertainment Capital of the World.

14 With me, everything is a gamble.

15 Wayne Newton calls me home.

16 My favorite and first bird was the flamingo.

17 I am the hot scene for the film *Oceans 11*.

18 Nicholas Cage won an Oscar® for leaving me.

19 My nickname is Lost Wages.

20 Jerry Tarkanian coached my local basketball team.

I am Las Vegas, Nevada.

2⊙ Questi⊙ns

INSTRUCT PLAYERS THAT "I AM A PLACE."

1 I am tropical.

2 I'm an island.

3 Christopher Columbus discovered me in 1492.

4 I am definitely not American.

5 Spanish is my official language.

6 I have a bay named after hoofed animals that roll in the mud.

7 I am the largest island in the West Indies.

8 Baseball has been very good to me.

9 I was once home to Hemingway.

10 I live on sugar.

11 *The Buena Vista Social Club* brought my music to the big screen.

12 I taught Ricky Ricardo how to play the drums.

13 In the 1970s and 1980s I assisted Soviet-supported movements.

14 I am known for my cigars.

15 Many of my people reside in Florida.

16 I had a missile crisis in JFK's days.

17 If you're a U.S. citizen, you probably haven't visited me.

18 The Pope came to visit me in 1998.

19 The U.S. has a long-standing embargo against me.

20 I won a famous custody battle in 2000.

I am Cuba.

2O Questions®

INSTRUCT PLAYERS THAT "I AM A PLACE."

1 My country has its own sea.

2 I am one of the most heavily populated places in the world.

3 My name used to be Edo.

4 One of my biggest holiday celebrations is Golden Week.

5 My heart is the Imperial Palace.

6 The Ginza District can be found inside me.

7 I am my nation's center for finance, communications and education.

8 The Bullet Train's first line included me.

9 My residents must provide proof of an off-street, overnight parking space to own a car.

10 I am not American.

11 I got bombed on April 18, 1942.

12 I hosted the 1964 Summer Olympic Games.

13 In March 1995, a religious cult gassed my subway system.

14 My Rose broadcasted during WWII.

15 I have streetcars and subways.

16 My people eat raw fish.

17 When Europeans first arrived in the 16th century, I was a small fishing village.

18 Jerry Lewis stars in a movie about my professional women.

19 My country is a world electronics leader.

20 I am Asian.

I am Tokyo, Japan.

2⊙ Qᵤₑₛₜⁱ⊙ₙₛ

INSTRUCT PLAYERS THAT "I AM A PLACE."

PLACES

1 I was born in 1971.
2 I am the home of Liberty Square.
3 I am twice the size of New York City.
4 I have a castle, but I'm not ruled by a king.
5 You will see lots of animals if you visit me.
6 I am in the U.S.
7 I'm located on 43 square miles of former swamp land.
8 I am one of the happiest places on earth.
9 I saw 10 million people in 1971.
10 My creator never saw me.
11 I am in the Sunshine State.
12 Every night I light up the sky.
13 You may go head over heels when you visit me.
14 I've got mice that aren't afraid of cats.
15 You can see Pluto when you visit me.
16 My entire town shuts down and is thoroughly cleaned every single night.
17 Las Vegas is the only place with more hotels than me.
18 I love to be visited by kids of all ages.
19 I am one of the most visited tourist attractions in the world.
20 I've got land in California.

I am Walt Disney World.

2O Questions®

INSTRUCT PLAYERS THAT "I AM A PLACE."

1 I have lots of cows and few people.
2 People visit me for hiking and fishing.
3 November 8, 1889 is a big date for me.
4 My flower is the bitterroot.
5 I am the 41st U.S. state.
6 I have seen lots of cowboys and Indians.
7 I had my share of gold rushes.
8 I saw Custer's Last Stand.
9 My capital is named after a woman.
10 I have the third lowest population density in the U.S.
11 I see the Continental Divide.
12 Jimmy Buffett sings about my Livingston.
13 Writer Thomas McGuane lives in me.
14 I have lots of dude ranches.
15 I border Canada.
16 I'm home to Glacier National Park.
17 The Dakotas border me.
18 Don't confuse me with a famous quarterback.
19 My name means "mountain" in Spanish.
20 My nickname is Big Sky Country.

I am Montana.

2O Questions®

INSTRUCT PLAYERS THAT "I AM A PLACE."

1 I am a country.

2 I've got a President.

3 I am north of the equator.

4 New Jersey and I are about the same size.

5 I became independent in 1948.

6 All of my men and unmarried women serve me.

7 I won the world's shortest war.

8 I'm not European or American.

9 My people buy things with shekels.

10 The U.S. is a friend to me.

11 I frequently make headlines.

12 My inhabitants can swim in the Mediterranean Sea.

13 I'm Middle Eastern.

14 I made Leon Uris famous.

15 If you know the Dead Sea, you know me.

16 My flag is blue and white.

17 I'm a good place to schmooze.

18 My laws are made in Parliament.

19 I have never been at peace with my neighbors.

20 I have been called Canaan and Palestine.

I am Israel.

2O Questions

INSTRUCT PLAYERS THAT "I AM A PLACE."

1 My climate is semi-tropical.
2 I have thousands of miles of water.
3 I'm American.
4 I became a state in 1812.
5 I am named for a king.
6 Rice is a major crop of mine.
7 I was the 18th state to join the U.S.
8 The Choctaw Indians were among my first inhabitants.
9 My Saints never met Roger Moore.
10 I am located in the South.
11 My nickname is the Pelican State.
12 Translated, my capital's name is "Red Stick."
13 I am the U.S. leader in shrimp production.
14 I border Texas.
15 The Mississippi River flows through me.
16 I was bought from the French in 1803.
17 I am shaped like a boot.
18 Huey Long is my Kingfish.
19 Many of my cooks are Cajun.
20 My largest city is home to the Sugar Bowl.

I am Louisiana.

2O Questions

INSTRUCT PLAYERS THAT "I AM A PLACE."

1 My climate is temperate.

2 I am a city.

3 You can find palm trees on my boulevards.

4 I am in North America.

5 My altitude is 7,350 feet.

6 I am located at the foot of two magnificent snow-covered volcanoes.

7 In 1551, the first university in North America was founded in me.

8 I hosted the Olympics in 1968.

9 My latitude is about the same as Bombay, India.

10 I have a population of over 25 million.

11 My subway system is called the Metro.

12 Cortez discovered me in 1519.

13 The Pyramid of the Sun is nearby.

14 My markets feature Indian arts and handicrafts.

15 The name of my country is in my name.

16 I was once the site of the capital city of the Aztec Empire.

17 Most of my inhabitants speak Spanish.

18 Montezuma's palace was located here.

19 Diego Rivera decorated my buildings.

20 I have a serious air pollution problem.

I am Mexico City, Mexico.

2O QuesTiONs

INSTRUCT PLAYERS THAT "I AM A PLACE."

1 I am American.
2 I am on the East Coast.
3 The Pilgrims gave me my start.
4 My Patriots aren't revolutionaries.
5 I'm named after the land of Queen Elizabeth.
6 I'm not a city, state or country.
7 I have excellent lobsters in my waters.
8 I know Paul Revere and Nathan Hale.
9 I'm home to many historic landmarks.
10 Despite my name, I am old.
11 I have more snow than the Southwest.
12 I have mountains and beaches.
13 I can see the Atlantic Ocean.
14 I have a popular soup named for me.
15 I have six members in my family.
16 The Brits helped name me.
17 I touch Canada.
18 Captain John Smith named me.
19 I was the center of the American Revolution.
20 I know Boston, but I don't know Chicago.

I am New England.

2O Questions®

INSTRUCT PLAYERS THAT "I AM A PLACE."

1 I am old and beautiful.

2 I am a country.

3 My Congress is a party.

4 I am home to over 200 languages.

5 I am Asian.

6 I touch the Arabian Sea and the Bay of Bengal.

7 I see the Himalayas every day.

8 Britain left me in 1947.

9 I've never broken a bone, but I am famous for my castes.

10 I can be a hot place to live.

11 In another life, my people may have been stones, flowers or cows.

12 Most of my people practice Hinduism.

13 Some of my residents are Sikh.

14 You'd be hard pressed to find beef in my Delhi.

15 Pakistan was carved out of me in 1934.

16 Only China has more people than me.

17 The Ganges River flows through me.

18 My people know curry.

19 My Taj Mahal is more than a casino.

20 I suffered from a major earthquake in 2001.

I am India.

2O Questions

INSTRUCT PLAYERS THAT "I AM A PLACE."

1 Columbus found me in 1493.

2 I am an autonomous commonwealth.

3 My population is overwhelmingly Roman Catholic.

4 Ponce de Leon colonized me.

5 Americans know me for my beaches and casinos.

6 To visit me, you'll likely come through the Luis Muñoz Marín International Airport.

7 I speak Spanish and English.

8 I sound a lot wealthier than I am.

9 I am surrounded by agua.

10 Some call me the Island of Enchantment.

11 My capital is named for St. John the Baptist.

12 I was ceded to the U.S. after the Spanish-American War.

13 I am the gateway from the Atlantic to the Caribbean.

14 Many of my citizens emigrate to New York.

15 My flag waves red, white and blue.

16 My people hold a yearly parade in New York City.

17 Maria of *West Side Story* calls me home.

18 Hurricane Hugo hit me in 1989.

19 I am home to Ricky Martin.

20 My PR has nothing to do with public relations.

I am Puerto Rico.

2O Questions

INSTRUCT PLAYERS THAT "I AM A PLACE."

1 I was important in 1864.

2 I was Marthasville and Terminus before I was me.

3 I am the largest city in my state.

4 My people eat at the Waffle House after midnight.

5 I'm 660 miles southwest of Washington, D.C.

6 I am the seat of Fulton County.

7 I have over twenty colleges and universities.

8 I am the capital of the Empire State of the South.

9 I'm six miles southeast of the Chatahoochie River.

10 Coca-Cola calls me home.

11 I'm near Stone Mountain and Six Flags.

12 I am home to Dr. Martin Luther King's Ebenezer Baptist Church.

13 *Gone With the Wind* author Margaret Mitchell hails from me.

14 Ted Turner has been a local resident of mine.

15 My Flames burn on ice.

16 My Braves aren't Indians.

17 I'm home to Hawks and Falcons.

18 My state is known for peaches and bulldogs.

19 I hosted the 1996 Summer Olympics.

20 My Georgia was never in the U.S.S.R.

I am Atlanta, Georgia.

2O Questions

INSTRUCT PLAYERS THAT "I AM A PLACE."

1   My water is over 80 degrees Fahrenheit.

2   I have white, sandy beaches.

3   My music beats to a different drum.

4   Harry Belafonte sang a farewell song about me.

5   I am a popular vacation spot for Americans.

6   I have "Royal" ports.

7   I was originally a Spanish colony.

8   None of my crops are indigenous to me.

9   Jimmy Cliff knows me well.

10   Rum punch is popular with my natives.

11   I am located in the Caribbean Sea.

12   Montego Bay is one of my hot spots.

13   My jerks have nothing to do with rude people.

14   I am made up of several islands.

15   My Olympic athletes were portrayed in the movie *Cool Runnings*.

16   I am Peter Tosh's home.

17   The Marley family made me famous.

18   I see more coconuts than corn.

19   Reggae is my music of choice.

20   Stella got her groove back while visiting me.

I am Jamaica.

2O Questions

INSTRUCT PLAYERS THAT "I AM A PLACE."

1 I was divided in 1920.

2 I am an island.

3 My people have been persecuted.

4 I am European.

5 Most of my people are Roman Catholic.

6 I'm home to the Cliffs of Moher.

7 Green and orange are my colors.

8 Cead Mille Failte is a motto of mine.

9 My beers can be stout.

10 My green is legendary.

11 I contain the Lakes of Killarney.

12 George Bernard Shaw is one of my natives.

13 My inhabitants make Waterford crystal.

14 According to legend, St. Patrick drove out all my snakes.

15 Some people call me Erin.

16 My eyes have been known to smile.

17 I suffered the Great Potato Famine.

18 My people are the mascot of Notre Dame University.

19 I am associated with leprechauns.

20 Kiss my Blarney Stone and you'll never be the same.

I am Ireland.

2O QUESTIONS

23

INSTRUCT PLAYERS THAT "I AM A PLACE."

PLACES

1 My currency is the shilling.

2 English and Swahili are my official languages.

3 I export tea, coffee and petroleum.

4 In 1998, the U.S. embassy was bombed in my capital city.

5 I am a former British colony.

6 I gained my independence in 1963.

7 Jomo Kenyatta was my first president.

8 My national football team is the Harambee Stars.

9 I am revered by many anthropologists as the "cradle of humanity."

10 I have tropical rainforests.

11 I'm home to Isak Dineson's farm.

12 I am located on the east coast of Africa.

13 Lake Victoria is located in me.

14 The Masai Mara is my finest wildlife sanctuary.

15 My capital is Nairobi.

16 I have snow-capped mountains.

17 William Holden and Stephanie Powers became enamored of me.

18 I am in the Southern Hemisphere.

19 I am a country.

20 I am famous for my long distance runners.

I am Kenya.

2O Questions

24

INSTRUCT PLAYERS THAT "I AM A PLACE."

1 I am a city.

2 You can find me in Europe.

3 I am the capital of my province.

4 I banned horses in 1392.

5 I'm famous for my glass.

6 I am joined to the mainland by bridges.

7 If you visit me, you might buy Chianti.

8 I have a piazza.

9 I have a bridge that's just your Sighs.

10 I have the Palace of the Doges.

11 My transportation system is all wet.

12 There is a beach in California named after me.

13 I'm at the top of the boot.

14 My currency used to be the lira.

15 Put on a mask and visit my Carnivale.

16 I am home to St. Mark's Cathedral.

17 I'm slowly sinking into the sea.

18 When you visit me you might ride in a gondola.

19 I am the site of the Rialto Bridge.

20 Shakespeare wrote about my merchant.

I am Venice, Italy.

2O Questions®

INSTRUCT PLAYERS THAT "I AM A PLACE."

PLACES

1 In the 1500s, Hernando De Soto explored me.

2 I am American.

3 In 1796, I became the 16th U.S. state.

4 I was the last state to secede from the union and the first to be readmitted.

5 Come to me and see Rock City.

6 Georgia and Missouri both border me.

7 I was once part of North Carolina.

8 My largest city sees Federal Express every night.

9 You can see seven states from me.

10 Davy Crockett served me in Congress.

11 Martin Luther King was assassinated in me.

12 You'll find the Great Smoky Mountains within me.

13 Andrew Jackson called me home.

14 I share my name with a famous American playwright.

15 I have three sets of double letters.

16 I'm known for my Volunteers.

17 Kentucky is one of my neighbors.

18 The Grateful Dead say "There ain't no place I'd rather be" than me.

19 I am home to Graceland.

20 My capital is the home of country music.

I am Tennessee.

2O Questions ®

INSTRUCT PLAYERS THAT "I AM A PLACE."

1 I have been on my own since 1961.
2 I am a country.
3 I was part of the Commonwealth.
4 I am in the Southern Hemisphere.
5 I have the most highly industrialized economy on my continent.
6 Cricket is one of my national pastimes.
7 I'm home to the Kalahari Desert.
8 I am African.
9 I know some real Boers.
10 I am a producer of diamonds.
11 English is my national language.
12 I am a major world producer of gold.
13 Namibia, Botswana and Zimbabwe are my neighbors.
14 Lesotho lies inside of me.
15 If you were marching to Pretoria, you'd be marching toward me.
16 I touch two oceans.
17 I contain Good Hope.
18 For me everything was black and white.
19 My largest city is named after Johan.
20 My apartheid policies were well known.

I am South Africa.

2O Questions

INSTRUCT PLAYERS THAT "I AM A PLACE."

1 I'm pretty oily.

2 My capital city is located at 40.78°N latitude.

3 I'm really salty.

4 I'm American.

5 One of my major cities is always Sandy.

6 From right to left, I include a hat.

7 My state bird is the California Gull.

8 I'm the Beehive State.

9 My motto is "Industry."

10 I am home to BYU.

11 I entered the Union on January 4, 1896.

12 I'm home to Rainbow Bridge.

13 I'm the 45th U.S. state.

14 I'm a leading producer of copper, gold, silver, lead and zinc.

15 The Osmond family calls me home.

16 I was the host of the 2002 Winter Olympics.

17 The Mormons settled my state capital.

18 My Jazz migrated from New Orleans.

19 I was named for the Ute Indians.

20 Scientists believe my famous lake was once an inland sea.

I am Utah.

2O Questions®

INSTRUCT PLAYERS THAT "I AM A PLACE."

1 I am located south of the equator.

2 I am an island.

0 I have world class windsurfing.

4 I'm not very big, but I have six volcanoes.

5 I am closer to Australia than to the U.S.

6 You might fly over Yap and Truk to get to me.

7 My people are largely Hindu.

8 I have monkey forests.

9 Terima kasih means "thank you" in my language.

10 The Dutch greatly influenced me.

11 I am home to Ngurah Rai International Airport.

12 Bob Hope and Bing Crosby visited me in one of the *Road* movies.

13 I'm in the Indian Ocean.

14 I am famous for my woodcarvings.

15 My cultural center is Ubud.

16 My famous dances feature handmade masks.

17 My currency is the rupee.

18 My beaches are in Kuta and Sanur.

19 Java is my neighbor.

20 I am in Indonesia.

I am Bali.

THINGS

2O Questions

INSTRUCT PLAYERS THAT "I AM A THING."

1 A lot of people fall for me.
2 I like winters better than summers.
3 I'll cost you quite a few greenbacks.
4 I'm not a biker, but I appreciate a good helmet.
5 I'm mostly flat but I do have a nice curve or two.
6 My popularity surged in the 1990s.
7 Ross Rebagliati won the gold medal at my Olympic premiere in 1998.
8 I am more popular with youngsters than oldsters.
9 I am required equipment in some sports events.
10 You'll find me at the X-Games.
11 I am a mode of transportation.
12 I love speed.
13 My binding has nothing to do with book publishing.
14 I get off on bumps, jumps and humps.
15 I get really psyched when I see a big mountain.
16 Some of my biggest advocates go surfing in the summer.
17 People stand on me when I'm doing my thing.
18 I'm not a smoker, but I get excited when I see a half pipe.
19 I am more than two feet long and less than seven feet long.
20 I am typically found at ski resorts, but I'm not skis.

I am a snowboard.

2⊙ Questions

INSTRUCT PLAYERS THAT "I AM A THING."

1   I am funny looking.

2   Africa is my native habitat.

3   My legs are long and powerful.

4   I can grow to be eight feet tall and can weigh up to 300 pounds.

5   My meat is a healthy alternative to hamburger.

6   I can run at speeds of up to 40 mph.

7   I hiss, but don't slither.

8   I dig a hole in sandy soil for a nest.

9   I eat many types of plants and seeds, as well as insects and lizards.

10   I swallow sand and stones.

11   I lay as many as ten eggs each season.

12   I usually live in open grassland areas.

13   I pretend to be injured if my nest and babies are threatened.

14   My eyes are bigger than my brain.

15   I cannot fly, but I'm a bird.

16   I have only two toes on each foot.

17   I am the largest of all living birds.

18   I have been raised on farms for my feather and leather.

19   My long neck and small head are featherless.

20   When I lay an egg, it's a biggie.

I am an ostrich.

2O Questions

INSTRUCT PLAYERS THAT "I AM A THING."

1. I am Asian.
2. I am popular with beginning pianists.
3. Some people find me hard to handle.
4. You won't find me in Thailand.
5. I got my start in the Shang Dynasty around 1766 B.C.
6. Sometimes I come with instructions.
7. I have a tapered physique.
8. Some people catch flies with me.
9. I am long and thin.
10. Like shoes, I come by the pair.
11. Sometimes women stick me in their hair.
12. Mulan used me in the Disney animated film.
13. I don't go with pizza or burgers.
14. I like eating.
15. My use requires fine motor skills.
16. I am usually made of wood or plastic.
17. Some people use me as drumsticks.
18. I'm a utensil.
19. I need you to lend me a hand.
20. People expect to see me in Chinese restaurants.

I am chopsticks.

2O Questions

INSTRUCT PLAYERS THAT "I AM A THING."

1 Rock stars and celebrities drop by to work with me on a weekly basis.
2 My grandma is named Jacqueline Bouvier.
3 My family has five members.
4 My favorite animal is a Fox.
5 My family shops at the Quickie Mart.
6 My aunts work at the DMV.
7 Sam Simon helps write my story.
8 Tracy Ullman gave me my start.
9 The head of my household works for a nuclear power plant.
10 My youngest member doesn't talk.
11 Jebediah Springfield founded my town.
12 Julie Kavner speaks for one of me.
13 Mr. Burns and Smithers like to boss one of me around.
14 I am a prime time TV series.
15 Santa's Little Helper is my family's best friend.
16 "Don't have a cow," guess now.
17 Matt Groening created me.
18 I've made an appearance at the Festival of Animation.
19 I am not related to O. J.
20 I have something in common with *The Flintstones*.

I am *The Simpsons.*

2O Questions

INSTRUCT PLAYERS THAT "I AM A THING."

1. I can be soft or firm.
2. I jiggle but I'm not Jell-O®.
3. I am sometimes silky, but I'm not a slip.
4. I was first made during the Han Dynasty.
5. I'm in fashion, but some say I have no taste.
6. I'm not a teacher, but sometimes I am a substitute.
7. I am popular with the Japanese.
8. I am a four-letter word.
9. I can be hot or cold.
10. I often come in a cube.
11. I am a food.
12. I'm good for your heart.
13. I'm not a flower, but I come from a plant.
14. There's an annual festival for me in Los Angeles, California.
15. I start out as a soybean.
16. I've been called a chameleon, even though I don't have four legs.
17. Some believe I can reduce the risk of cancer.
18. I am high in protein.
19. You'll find me in miso soup.
20. I am known as "the meat without bones."

I am tofu.

2O Quⅇsti⊙ns

INSTRUCT PLAYERS THAT "I AM A THING."

1 I was on the cover of *Time* magazine in 1975.

2 I started at the Police Academy in Los Angeles.

3 I aired on ABC.

4 I am a detective series.

5 I first aired in 1974.

6 I was originally called *The Alley Cats*.

7 I'm baaaack. Get out your curling iron.

8 I take place in Los Angeles.

9 I got my start as a TV show.

10 John Forsythe spoke for me.

11 One of my original members is a famous poster girl.

12 Aaron Spelling is my producer.

13 Jill, Sabrina and Kelly are my originals.

14 My movie debuted in 2000 with martial arts and high tech stunts.

15 My stars are employed at Townsend Detective Agency.

16 I have angels but no devils.

17 Drew Barrymore brought me to the big screen.

18 Bill Murray played the male lead in my first movie.

19 My Charlie isn't a chaplain.

20 My cast includes three female detectives and a never-seen boss.

I am *Charlie's Angels*.

20 QUESTIONS

INSTRUCT PLAYERS THAT "I AM A THING."

1 I can wreak havoc.

2 I can rock and roll.

3 I am a stress releaser.

4 I bring people together in times of tragedy.

5 I am loud and I wave when I come.

6 I am natural.

7 People try to predict my arrival.

8 I make the news.

9 Despite my strength, people focus on my faults.

10 I tend to break things.

11 I shake people up.

12 When I arrive, run to the nearest exit but don't leave.

13 Cities are planned with me in mind.

14 I can bring down the house.

15 If I am big, you can hear me roar.

16 I happen about a million times each year.

17 San Franciscans remember me for my visits in 1906 and 1989.

18 El Salvador, India and Seattle, Washington suffered from me in 2001.

19 Geologists are obsessed with me.

20 If you want to know how big I am, use a Richter scale.

I am an earthquake.

2O Questions

INSTRUCT PLAYERS THAT "I AM A THING."

1 I go on lots of vacations.
2 I can be good or bad.
3 I can be old, new, borrowed or blue.
4 I'm bound to be seen.
5 I am a four-letter word.
6 If I'm good, you'll stick with me.
7 A lot of people take me to bed.
8 College students hit me.
9 I include a table but no chairs.
10 I can be full of religion, romance or recipes.
11 I come with a spine but no backbone.
12 I'm full of words but I never talk.
13 I had a pressing engagement with Gutenberg.
14 Sometimes I'm banned.
15 Buildings are erected to hold me.
16 I'm dedicated.
17 I can put you to sleep.
18 I'm black and white and often read.
19 Oprah started a club for me.
20 Trees die for me.

I am a book.

2O Questions

INSTRUCT PLAYERS THAT "I AM A THING."

1 I'm a rectangular prism.

2 I go camping a lot.

3 I don't occur naturally.

4 I've served in several wars.

5 I come in a can.

6 I'm an original convenience food.

7 I'm not usually served in restaurants.

8 People often poke fun at me, but there's not much I "can" do about it.

9 I'm edible—honest.

10 I helped make *Monty Python* a hit.

11 I can show up at breakfast, lunch or dinner.

12 No one could confuse me with haute cuisine.

13 I'm a four-letter word.

14 My name includes "spa," but I'm no health food.

15 I'm full of meat.

16 You may need a key to use me.

17 Hormel gave me my start in 1937.

18 Rearrange my letters and I spell "maps."

19 I'm quite a ham.

20 In 2000, Bepuzzled made me into a puzzle.

I am Spam®.

2O Questions

10

INSTRUCT PLAYERS THAT "I AM A THING."

1 I am always a scheduled event.
2 John Locke wrote about me in his "Second Treatise on Government".
3 My announcements lead to some great partying.
4 My booth has nothing to do with eating at the coffee shop.
5 In the U.S., Tuesday is my favorite day of the week.
6 My results end up in the newspaper and sometimes on TV.
7 I am an infrequent event in most countries in the world.
8 I can be very local or I can include the entire country.
9 In America, less than fifty percent of the people take part in me.
10 In ancient Greece, the polis guaranteed that every man participated in me.
11 In 2000, my mishandling left the world laughing at the United States.
12 I am considered a basic right.
13 In America, I am as regular as the summer Olympics.
14 People have been fighting for the right to have me for centuries.
15 The pollsters are busy before my appearance.
16 Abraham Lincoln needed me in order to become president.
17 Most Americans first experience me in student council.
18 I am a government project.
19 Politicians couldn't exist without me.
20 I help people select leaders.

I am an election.

2O Questions

11

INSTRUCT PLAYERS THAT "I AM A THING."

1 I am a landmark.

2 I am a technological masterpiece.

3 I am bigger than a breadbox.

4 It took almost 27 months to build me.

5 I have 2.5 million rivets.

6 I am man-made.

7 You could say I'm well composed; I have 12,000 parts.

8 I celebrate the anniversary of a revolution.

9 I am a great tourist attraction.

10 My lights add to my city's reputation.

11 When I was first erected, many thought I was an eyesore.

12 I bear my creator's name.

13 I was built in the 19th century.

14 I am wrought of iron.

15 I have a radio antenna on my top.

16 I'm a European icon.

17 There's a mini-me in Las Vegas.

18 I'm French, but I completely overlook Paris.

19 I sit by the Seine River.

20 I've got a great gift shop and café.

I am the Eiffel Tower.

20 Questions

INSTRUCT PLAYERS THAT "I AM A THING."

1 I have few enemies.
2 I resemble my southern relatives.
3 I blend in with my surroundings.
4 Few have seen me in my natural habitat.
5 I'm a good swimmer.
6 I rarely live past age 15.
7 I can weigh up to a ton.
8 I am a mammal.
9 I am a favorite at the zoo.
10 I have a whale of an appetite.
11 If I took my coat off, you'd see that my skin is black.
12 I am carnivorous.
13 I'm not Rip Van Winkle, but I take long naps.
14 I own a fur coat.
15 I sleep in a den.
16 The colder, the better, as far as I'm concerned.
17 I always wear white.
18 My cubs aren't scouts.
19 I symbolize the Arctic.
20 You'll have to bear with me.

I am a polar bear.

2⦿ Questions

INSTRUCT PLAYERS THAT "I AM A THING."

1 People tend to dress up for me.

2 I go on day and night.

3 I'm followed by a lot of headaches.

4 My parades aren't known for their roses.

5 Dionysius would feel at home with me.

6 My krewes don't row boats.

7 I'm one of the world's biggest parties.

8 My colors are purple, green and gold.

9 I'm Fat.

10 In Rio, I'm known as Carnival.

11 I throw beads and necklaces into the streets.

12 When I take over the Quarter, the whole town celebrates.

13 I've seen a lot of hurricanes, but not so much wind.

14 My floats aren't made with ice cream.

15 To many, I'm quite jazzy.

16 I'm followed by Ash Wednesday.

17 Tuesday is my day. Let's party.

18 Rum and bourbon help define my annual ritual.

19 I don't live in the jungle, but I'm wild.

20 I'm associated with New Orleans.

I am Mardi Gras.

2O Questions

INSTRUCT PLAYERS THAT "I AM A THING."

1. I like my own space.
2. I know Asians, African Americans and Russians.
3. I take about an hour at a time.
4. I have a doctor with me at all times.
5. I have been on TV and in the movies.
6. I have been around since 1965.
7. I have a cult following.
8. Sometimes I can't believe my ears.
9. I take you to new places where no man has gone before.
10. Certain crystals empower me.
11. I see stars and planets no scientist has ever witnessed.
12. There is a whole new generation of me.
13. John Belushi and Dan Ackroyd made fun of me.
14. Although not a business, my Enterprise keeps me going.
15. If you know Jean-Luc Picard, you know my story.
16. I am not real.
17. My Voyager has a female skipper.
18. My ships don't travel by sea.
19. I am the story of a mission.
20. I take place in the future.

I am *Star Trek.*

2O Questions

INSTRUCT PLAYERS THAT "I AM A THING."

1 Sometimes, I'm quite alarming.
2 People like it when I'm on time.
3 Sometimes I wear bells.
4 I have my own circular logic.
5 I'm a machine.
6 I've never been convicted of murder but I've been accused of killing time.
7 I like to sit by your bed.
8 I get punched out at work.
9 My hours are numbered.
10 I have two hands but no legs.
11 I could be a grandfather, but not a grandson.
12 Wait a second—sometimes I have three hands.
13 I'm not a TV, but sometimes people watch me.
14 You can find me in a VCR, a car and a microwave oven.
15 I have a great memory when the lights go out.
16 I'm related to a sundial.
17 My face has no eyes and no expression.
18 I can be digital.
19 I like to hang out on walls.
20 I get excited when I'm all wound up.

I am a clock.

2O Questions

INSTRUCT PLAYERS THAT "I AM A THING."

1 I'm an American institution.
2 I'm usually delivered.
3 I help raise money for a good cause.
4 I come in a box.
5 I only come around once a year.
6 I sometimes end up in the freezer.
7 I'm always associated with females.
8 I've seen a lot of milk in my time.
9 If you know Trefoil, you know me.
10 You can't find me in supermarkets.
11 My peanut butter doesn't come with jelly.
12 Despite my name, I'm made for boys, too.
13 I'm a dieter's nightmare.
14 My girls wear green.
15 My lemons aren't sour.
16 My girls wear uniforms.
17 I can satisfy your sweet tooth.
18 I'm sold door-to-door.
19 When I'm thin, I'm minty.
20 My providers started as Guides; now they're Scouts.

I am Girl Scout® Cookies.

2O Questions

INSTRUCT PLAYERS THAT "I AM A THING."

1. People talk about me a lot, but they don't come right up and say "Hi."
2. I am hard to find in Antarctica.
3. I have been in the news.
4. I'm totally far out.
5. The more you use your refrigerator, the thinner I get.
6. Once I'm gone, I can't be replaced.
7. I hate aerosol sprays.
8. I have a hole.
9. I'm not made by humans.
10. I don't eat beans, but I'm full of gas.
11. I am a layer that you won't find in any cake.
12. I get higher than the clouds.
13. I am made of oxygen.
14. I am in the stratosphere.
15. Chlorofluorocarbons destroy me.
16. My demise leads to skin cancer and crop damage.
17. Environmentalists are concerned about losing me.
18. I shield the earth from ultraviolet radiation.
19. I am necessary for human survival.
20. You can't talk about global warming without mentioning me.

I am the ozone layer.

2O Questions

INSTRUCT PLAYERS THAT "I AM A THING."

1   My Rome is not from Italy.
2   You shouldn't play with my Jacks on the floor.
3   I'm sweet.
4   A famous Johnny knows me well.
5   My history dates back to biblical times.
6   I'm no stranger to lunchboxes.
7   I spin on Beatles albums.
8   I can be red, green, pink or yellow.
9   My Grannies aren't old.
10 My pie has nothing to do with 3.14159.
11 I've been known to keep doctors away.
12 I may show up in a pig's mouth.
13 If you like me, I could be "of your eye."
14 When I get smashed, I really get sauced.
15 Unlike money, I grow on trees.
16 Sometimes people get confused and compare me to oranges.
17 My skin has a peel.
18 I helped Isaac Newton discover gravity.
19 I am often paired with Adam's.
20 I'm a real fruit.

I am an apple.

2O QUESTIONS

19

INSTRUCT PLAYERS THAT "I AM A THING."

THINGS

1 I use only one vowel.

2 I show up around the world.

3 Spell me with an "a" and I really rock.

4 I'm found outside.

5 I fly.

6 The ancient Egyptians revered me.

7 I'm an automotive legend.

8 You might get slugged if you don't spot me on the road.

9 I share my name with a popular German car.

10 I can be a real pest.

11 With Paul and John, I started out silver.

12 I've been known to eat dung.

13 I crawl.

14 Gardeners fear me.

15 There are many types of me, including carpet, wood and leather.

16 I'm afraid of Raid®.

17 David Ogilvy called me a lemon.

18 I eat plants.

19 I sound like I belong with Paul McCartney, but my wings are actually used for flying.

20 The largest of my kind weighs about 3.5 ounces.

I am a beetle.

2O Questions

INSTRUCT PLAYERS THAT "I AM A THING."

1 I'm a Razor, but I have no blade.
2 I'm back in vogue after decades of being ignored.
3 Sometimes I have a motor.
4 My wheels can be colorful.
5 My bunny hops aren't performed by bunnies.
6 I've been banned from some schoolyards.
7 I can be folded up and put into a backpack.
8 I'm usually silver.
9 I brake a lot, but don't need to be fixed.
10 You'll love to handle my bars.
11 I'm powered by human feet.
12 I'm a mode of transportation.
13 I have wheels.
14 I can be a status symbol for kids.
15 Sometimes I have lights and shock absorbers.
16 I'm sold in toy stores.
17 I am a six-letter word.
18 I'm not as fast as a car or a bike.
19 My nasty falls don't include water.
20 I'm usually found outdoors.

I am a scooter.

2O Questions

21

INSTRUCT PLAYERS THAT "I AM A THING."

1. You don't have to plug me in to get power.
2. Black is my favorite color.
3. My focus is your focus.
4. I am always referred to in the plural.
5. My case has nothing to do with lawyers.
6. I don't care if the pupils I work with go to school.
7. I've got two barrels but I'm not a gun.
8. Police use me in stakeouts.
9. My straps make it easy for me to hang around.
10. Without a good lens, I can't make contact.
11. I believe that two eyes are better than one.
12. My eyesight is better than 20/20.
13. I've been to more operas than the fat lady has.
14. I can be part of a visual identification system.
15. I can make things look closer to you or farther away.
16. I've been to a lot of football games.
17. I have something in common with a microscope.
18. I like to go bird watching.
19. People like me because I make things big.
20. My scope is far and wide.

I am binoculars.

20 Questions

22

INSTRUCT PLAYERS THAT "I AM A THING."

1 I am open 24 hours a day.
2 The first of my kind was opened in Massachusetts in 1654.
3 I employ a lot of people.
4 I am usually run by the state.
5 I don't have a fence but I often have a gate.
6 You may have read about my *Phantom*.
7 My money often ends up in the streets.
8 Sometimes I come at the beginning of a long span.
9 There is a type of cookie that shares my first name.
10 I've been known to hold up traffic.
11 My tokens are more than just tokens.
12 People pass through me every day.
13 I make you stop but I'm not a traffic light.
14 Sometimes I will give you a ticket.
15 My plaza doesn't have shops.
16 I am a booth but I'm not found in restaurants.
17 I am usually found on a highway.
18 I'll charge you $5 to cross the Golden Gate Bridge.
19 People often throw money at me.
20 In New York, I stand right before the tunnels.

I am a tollbooth.

2O Questions

23

INSTRUCT PLAYERS THAT "I AM A THING."

1. People want me.
2. Bob Pittman got me started.
3. I made stars of Martha Quinn and Kennedy. Remember them?
4. I'm known for my stylish house.
5. *Remote Control* was my first game show.
6. My cables won't start cars.
7. I got going in the early 1980s.
8. My name is always abbreviated.
9. I've seen Bill Clinton play the saxophone.
10. I'm an icon of pop culture.
11. My Carson never hosted *The Tonight Show*.
12. I supported Randee for President in 1988.
13. I moved to Times Square in the 1990s.
14. I popularized Cyndi Lauper and Culture Club in the early days.
15. Teenagers love to watch me.
16. I observe *Road Rules*.
17. I can tell you the *100 Best Pop Songs*.
18. I'm part of the *Real World*.
19. I host my own music awards.
20. I play music but have no DJs.

I am MTV.

2O Questions

24

INSTRUCT PLAYERS THAT "I AM A THING."

1. I got started in 1951, in a bathroom in New York.
2. I'm an American legend.
3. Kids love to play with me.
4. A black box got me going.
5. I really stick to it.
6. The French say I offer infinite sticking pleasure.
7. I show up in play sets, games, puzzles and books.
8. I was one of the first toys to be advertised on TV.
9. I've appeared with Barbie®, Mickey Mouse and Harry Potter.
10. Preschoolers love me.
11. I'm made of static-cling vinyl.
12. More than one billion of my play sets have been sold.
13. I was acquired by University Games in 1998.
14. I know Pete, Penny and Miss Weather.
15. I'm thin and colorful.
16. If you make a mistake with me, just lift and start again.
17. I'm in the Toy Hall of Fame.
18. I'm known for creating a scene.
19. I'm a well-known creativity tool.
20. In 2001, I celebrated my 50th birthday at FAO Schwarz.

I am Colorforms®.

2O Questions

25

INSTRUCT PLAYERS THAT "I AM A THING."

1 I am Italian.
2 I have black hair and dark eyes.
3 I've spent lots of time alone with a Prince (in his bathroom).
4 I'm told that I look like the second wife of Francesco del Giocondo.
5 I like to sit.
6 I am art.
7 People come to visit me every day except Tuesday.
8 I am the subject of songs and movies.
9 The French call me "La Gioconda."
10 Some say I am a female version of my creator.
11 My secrets keep me smiling.
12 I am a famous Renaissance work of art.
13 I was finished in 1506.
14 I live behind glass.
15 I am more oil than water.
16 I'm only 30.5" x 20.9", but I have a big reputation.
17 I hang around the Louvre.
18 I am a painting.
19 I've been copied but never reproduced.
20 Leonardo da Vinci created me.

I am the Mona Lisa.

2O Questions

26

INSTRUCT PLAYERS THAT "I AM A THING."

1 I need to get charged up every day to do my thing.
2 I've been called a public nuisance.
3 I have good hearing.
4 My ancestors often stayed by your bed or in the kitchen.
5 I can be a lifesaver in an emergency.
6 *E.T.* would have been much shorter if I was around.
7 I've been known to distract drivers.
8 I might die on you.
9 Some speculate that I cause cancer.
10 Despite my name, I have nothing to do with molecular biology.
11 I can go almost anywhere that you go.
12 Black is my favorite color.
13 I can play games with you.
14 I like to be turned on.
15 I'm usually banned on airplanes.
16 I can reconnect you with your mother.
17 The most common word that I hear is "Hello."
18 I might not always give you a great reception.
19 I fit in your back pocket.
20 In England, I'm mobile.

I am a cellular phone.

2O Questions

27

INSTRUCT PLAYERS THAT "I AM A THING."

1 I'm tall for my age.
2 I have stories that can't be told.
3 Superman can fly higher than me.
4 My flights are not on an airplane.
5 I have 3,194,547 light bulbs.
6 I took seven million man-hours to build.
7 I was completed in 1931.
8 Each year, I am struck by lightning more than 100 times.
9 I am closest to the N, R, B, D, F & Q.
10 I know Cary Grant and King Kong.
11 I have been the site of an annual vertical race since 1978.
12 I have 73 elevators.
13 In 1945, a plane crashed into me.
14 I play a pivotal role in *An Affair to Remember*.
15 I am located at 350 Fifth Avenue.
16 You can see me from New Jersey.
17 My initials are E.S.B.
18 I scrape the sky.
19 Tourists find me quite attractive.
20 I am in New York City.

I am the Empire State Building.

2O Questions®

28

INSTRUCT PLAYERS THAT "I AM A THING."

1 I'm big on Bourbon Street.

2 I spend most of my time out at sea.

3 I always travel at speeds exceeding 70 mph.

4 I visit Florida, Georgia and the Carolinas annually.

5 For decades I was named after girls, even though I'm not female.

6 I can be a drink and a type of glass.

7 My cane isn't used for walking.

8 In Tulsa, I'm Golden.

9 When I pass my wind, watch out.

10 I am the promenade deck on an ocean liner.

11 I am a weather condition.

12 I can be more destructive than war or famine.

13 I have my own season every year in the southeastern U.S.

14 Extreme flooding often follows me.

15 I am boxer Rueben Carter's nickname.

16 My weaker little brother is a real cyclone.

17 I'm often composed of rain, thunder and lighting.

18 People fear me because of my destructive personality.

19 My closest inland relative is the tornado.

20 Believe it or not, I've been known to stop the U.S. Postal Service.

I am a hurricane.

YEARS

2O Questions

INSTRUCT PLAYERS THAT "I AM A YEAR."

1 Spain joined NATO before I ended.
2 I read the debut issue of *USA Today*.
3 My World's Fair was in Knoxville.
4 I ended AT&T's U.S. telephone monopoly.
5 I gave John Updike a Pulitzer Prize.
6 I saw the Equal Rights Amendment fail.
7 I witnessed a war in the Falkland Islands.
8 I saw *Family Ties* start its long TV run.
9 I wanted my MTV.
10 I saw seven people die from taking Tylenol laced with cyanide.
11 I first saw Andrew Lloyd Webber's musical *Cats*.
12 I saw the Cardinals beat the Brewers in the World Series.
13 I premiered *E.T.* at the movies.
14 I first saw Kodak's disc camera.
15 I got a peek at Dustin Hoffman in drag in the movie *Tootsie*.
16 Italy took home my World Cup.
17 I gave Barney Clark the first artificial heart.
18 I dedicated the Vietnam Veteran's Memorial in Washington, D.C.
19 I saw John Belushi's fatal drug overdose.
20 I saw the birth of England's Prince William.

I am 1982.

2⊙ Que**st**i⊙ns®

INSTRUCT PLAYERS THAT "I AM A YEAR."

1   I saw Jane Goodall establish a Tanzanian research camp.

2   I saw the Lakers move to Los Angeles.

3   I saw dancers twist to Chubby Checker's hit.

4   I checked out the surf during the Chilean tsunami.

5   I saw France acquire atomic capability.

6   I heard Frank Sinatra's *Swingin' Session*.

7   I saw Gary Powers' U2 shot down.

8   I was at JFK's inauguration.

9   I saw people get a little *Psycho* about taking showers.

10 I saw two U.S. Navy Frogmen become the first to reach the Marianas Trench.

11 The Chinese think I'm a rat.

12 Dwight D. Eisenhower was my U.S. president.

13 I saw Yul Brynner in *The Magnificent Seven*.

14 I'm a great year, but I end in a zero.

15 My Olympics were held in Rome.

16 I saw Spencer Tracy in *Inherit the Wind*.

17 I saw the Soviets launch two dogs into orbit in Sputnik 5.

18 I saw the opening of *Camelot* on Broadway.

19 The FDA approved the Pill during my time.

20 The Pirates won my World Series.

I am 1960.

2⊙ Que{ti⊙n{

INSTRUCT PLAYERS THAT "I AM A YEAR."

1 I saw NATO go to war over human rights violations in Kosovo.

2 I witnessed a judge find Microsoft to be a monopoly.

3 I heard Monica Lewinsky become a household name.

4 Prince sings a song about me.

5 I said goodbye to Stanley Kubrick.

6 I never really caught the Y2K bug.

7 I had *The Sixth Sense*.

8 I launched the Latin Invasion.

9 I saw the Broncos in the Super Bowl.

10 I saw Hillary Clinton run for the U.S. Senate.

11 Some believed the world was going to end when I did.

12 I experienced the tragedy of the Columbine school shootings.

13 I saw JFK Jr. die in a plane crash.

14 I saw the Yankees win the World Series.

15 I saw the first non-stop, non-refueled balloon fly around the world.

16 I said goodbye to Joe DiMaggio.

17 Atlanta lost my Super Bowl and World Series.

18 I saw Delaware get its own quarter.

19 I'm the last of my kind.

20 I was first to see Pokémon™ cards traded.

I am 1999.

2O QueStioNs

INSTRUCT PLAYERS THAT "I AM A YEAR."

1 Hawaii and Alaska were not states during me.
2 The first jet aircraft flew for seven minutes during my August.
3 Gangster Al Capone was paroled in my time.
4 I read the first Batman comic.
5 I heard Dorothy say "There's no place like home."
6 I licked the first U.S. food stamp.
7 I saw the British passenger ship Athenia sink.
8 Lou Gehrig retired during me.
9 I heard Ghandi call on the world to disarm.
10 I hosted the World's Fair in New York.
11 I put Major League Baseball on TV.
12 I first read about the Joad family.
13 I made Bobby Riggs a winner at Wimbeldon.
14 Stalin was named *Time's* "Man of the Year" during me.
15 *Pinocchio* was a disappointment at the box office during my time.
16 I saw the first regular airline passenger service between the U.S. and Europe.
17 Roosevelt became the first U.S. president to appear on TV in my time.
18 I witnessed Germany invade Poland.
19 I premiered the movie version of *Gone with the Wind*.
20 I am thirty-something.

I am 1939.

20 Questions

INSTRUCT PLAYERS THAT "I AM A YEAR."

1. My U.S. president was Eisenhower.
2. I saw the first U.S. atomic submarine launched.
3. I saw Marilyn Monroe wed Joe DiMaggio.
4. I saw Earl Warren become Chief Justice of the Supreme Court.
5. I saw the Lakers win my NBA championship.
6. I saw Charles Lindbergh win the Pulitzer Prize for *The Spirit of St.Louis*.
7. I saw crew cuts and flattops become cool.
8. I saw New York win the World Series.
9. I saw the premier of TV's *Father Knows Best*.
10. I saw the first televised Cabinet meeting.
11. I saw Democrats regain both houses of Congress.
12. I saw the premiere of *Face the Nation* on TV.
13. I saw Mays and Berra both win MVPs.
14. I saw the Supreme Court issue the ruling in Brown vs. Board of Education that led to school desegregation.
15. My favorite movie is *On the Waterfront*.
16. I saw the U.S. license the first polio vaccine.
17. I watched the World Series broadcast in color for the first time.
18. I saw Lee Petty win the Winston Cup.
19. I heard "under God" added to the Pledge of Allegiance.
20. I saw the birth of Ron Howard.

I am 1954.

2O Questions

INSTRUCT PLAYERS THAT "I AM A YEAR."

1 My 00 doesn't come before seven.

2 I saw Sigmund Freud's *The Interpretation of Dreams* published.

3 I was the first to read L. Frank Baum's *The Wonderful Wizard of Oz*.

4 I charged 2¢ for a U.S. stamp.

5 I saw Montreal win the Stanley Cup.

6 Blanche Hillyard won my Wimbledon.

7 I watched the Summer Olympics in Paris.

8 I was there when Lefty Grove was born.

9 The Boxer Rebellion in China occurred during my time.

10 I was the first to see the Eiffel Tower.

11 I attended McKinley's second election.

12 Theodore Roosevelt was my Vice President.

13 I saw Booker T. Washington organize the National Negro Business League.

14 I saw more than 8,000 cars on U.S. roads.

15 I saw construction begin on the New York Subway.

16 I signaled the start of a new age.

17 I saw train engineer Casey Jones sacrifice his life to save his passengers.

18 I saw J.C. Penny open his first Golden Rule Store in Kemmerer, Wyoming.

19 I saw the first Brownie box camera.

20 I watched the Paris Exposition celebrate the arrival of a new century.

I am 1900.

20 Questions

INSTRUCT PLAYERS THAT "I AM A YEAR."

YEARS

1 I am from the 20th century.
2 The U.S. economy was booming during me; the Asian market was a bust.
3 I never saw World War II.
4 You were definitely alive during me.
5 I watched Jay Leno host *The Tonight Show*.
6 Bill Clinton was my president.
7 The New York Yankees won my World Series.
8 I found Furby® fabulous.
9 I saw Seinfeld go off the air.
10 I witnessed the first live birth on the Internet.
11 *Forbes* magazine called Bill Gates the richest man in the world during my time.
12 I watched Teletubbies toddle onto TV screens around the U.S.
13 I heard the Spice Girls top the pop charts in the U.S.
14 I read about Monica Lewinsky and Ken Starr all summer.
15 I saw Northern Ireland sign a peace agreement.
16 *There's Something About Mary* was a huge hit at the box office in my time.
17 Mark McGwire knocked a record seventy home runs out of the park during me.
18 I saw Peyton Manning join the Indianapolis Colts.
19 Gwyneth Paltrow won her first Academy Award® during my time.
20 The sum of my digits is more than 24 and less than 30.

I am 1998.

2O Questions

INSTRUCT PLAYERS THAT "I AM A YEAR."

1 I finished a World War.
2 Bebop was all the rage in my time.
3 I synthesized Vitamin A.
4 I saw the United Nations Charter signed.
5 I saw photographer Alfred Eisenstaedt capture a famous kiss in Times Square.
6 The U.S. welcomed its "boys" home from overseas during me.
7 I added fluoride to water.
8 I saw De Gaulle elected in France.
9 I witnessed U.S. troops liberate the concentration camp at Dachau.
10 Mussolini was shot during my time.
11 I read Orwell's *Animal Farm*.
12 I watched Hitchcock's *Spellbound*.
13 I rocked Neil Young in a baby cradle.
14 President Roosevelt died during me.
15 I saw the Arab League form against the establishment of a Jewish state.
16 I am not a leap year.
17 I saw the only offensive use of nuclear weapons.
18 I began the Nuremberg trials.
19 Harry Truman became president during me.
20 I retired Rosie the Riveter.

I am 1945.

20 QUESTIONS

INSTRUCT PLAYERS THAT "I AM A YEAR."

1 I saw Bruce Jenner win the decathlon.

2 I saw Howard Hughes die.

3 *A Chorus Line* won a Tony in my time.

4 I gave birth to Apple Computer.

5 I retired Hank Aaron.

6 I saw the Celtics beat the Suns for the NBA title.

7 I premiered the film *All the President's Men*.

8 *Rocky* was a knockout at the box office in my time.

9 I watched Chris Evert win Wimbeldon.

10 I saw Vietnam united.

11 I awarded Saul Bellow the Nobel Prize in Literature.

12 My Fourth of July was the biggest celebration of its kind in a hundred years.

13 The Reds defeated the Yankees in my World Series.

14 Mao Tse-tung died during me.

15 My February had 29 days.

16 I am post-Nixon and pre-Reagan.

17 I saw Jimmy Carter elected president.

18 I witnessed the kidnapping of a school bus full of children in Chowchilla, CA.

19 *King Kong* bombed at the box office in my time.

20 Nadia Comaneci earned the Olympics' first perfect gymnastics score in my time.

I am 1976.

2O Questions

INSTRUCT PLAYERS THAT "I AM A YEAR."

1 I am not an election year.
2 I heard Allen Ginsberg use the term "flower power."
3 I saw NASA launch Early Bird.
4 I read Ralph Nader's *Unsafe at Any Speed*.
5 Winston Churchill died in my time.
6 I saw the first cigarette packages printed with health warnings.
7 *The Sound of Music* won my Academy Award® for Best Picture.
8 I watched *I Dream of Jeannie* debut on ABC.
9 I saw Malcolm X assassinated.
10 I got a peek at the first miniskirt in London.
11 I heard The Grateful Dead play.
12 I read Norman Mailer's *An American Dream*.
13 I brought pretty baby Brooke Shields into the world.
14 I saw marching to Montgomery, Alabama.
15 I witnessed the first university teach-ins protesting the war in Vietnam.
16 I heard talk of the "Great Society."
17 I am not a leap year.
18 I heard the Beatles cry "Help!"
19 Lyndon Johnson was my president.
20 I saw riots in Watts in Los Angeles.

I am 1965.

2O Questions

INSTRUCT PLAYERS THAT "I AM A YEAR."

1 I saw Henry Ford purchase the Wright Brothers' old bicycle shop.

2 I saw Babe Ruth enter the Baseball Hall of Fame.

3 I read *How to Win Friends and Influence People*.

4 My Olympic Games were held in Berlin.

5 Jesse Owens starred in my Olympics.

6 The first issue of *Life* magazine was published during my time.

7 Abbie Hoffman was born in my time.

8 Franco's fascist troops invaded Spain in my July.

9 I read *Gone with the Wind* for the first time.

10 I introduced Flash Gordon to America.

11 I welcomed the United Auto Workers Union.

12 I saw the first commercial flight from the mainland to Hawaii.

13 I saw Heinrich Himmler become the head of the Gestapo.

14 I saw the first flight of the Hindenberg.

15 Rudyard Kipling died during my time.

16 I saw the birth of Jim Henson.

17 I am a leap year.

18 I'm near the middle of my decade.

19 F.D.R. was my U.S. president.

20 I witnessed King Edward VIII abdicate his throne to marry Wallis Warfield Simpson.

I am 1936.

2O QUESTIONS®

INSTRUCT PLAYERS THAT "I AM A YEAR."

1 I saw labor unrest begin in Poland.

2 Rhodesia became Zimbabwe in my time.

3 I saw Mount St. Helens blow.

4 The Supreme Court ruled that living organisms can be patented during me.

5 I viewed the Picasso Retrospective at the Museum of Modern Art in New York.

6 I saw the birth of the Walkman® and Post-It Notes®.

7 I said goodbye to Mae West.

8 I watched Walter Cronkite retire from CBS.

9 *Coal Miner's Daughter* was at the movies during me.

10 *Solid Gold* kicked off its TV run during me.

11 I saw the Shah of Iran die in Egypt.

12 The Phillies won my World Series.

13 Clint Eastwood filmed *Any Which Way You Can* during me.

14 I heard Americans ask, "Who shot J. R.?"

15 I saw John Lennon assassinated.

16 I elected Reagan president.

17 The U.S. ice hockey team won its 2nd Olympic gold medal in my time.

18 My Academy Awards® were postponed because of an assassination attempt on the President.

19 The Lakers scored my NBA title.

20 Moscow hosted my Olympics.

I am 1980.

2O Questions

INSTRUCT PLAYERS THAT "I AM A YEAR."

1 I saw the rock musical *Hair*.

2 I witnessed a bloody riot at the Democratic Convention in Chicago.

3 The Detroit Tigers beat the St. Louis Cardinals in my World Series.

4 I saw the first African American woman elected to Congress.

5 Martin Luther King, Jr. died during my time.

6 I saw The Doors and Steppenwolf release new albums.

7 I heard the *60 Minutes* clock start ticking.

8 France hosted my Winter Olympics.

9 I saw Turn in Your Draft Card Day.

10 I dedicated the Gateway Arch in St. Louis.

11 I saw Robert Kennedy assassinated.

12 I watched *2001: A Space Odyssey* years ahead of its time.

13 I saw Barbra Streisand and Katharine Hepburn share the Best Actress Oscar®.

14 I am a leap year.

15 I witnessed Jacqueline Kennedy and Aristotle Onassis head down the aisle.

16 My Summer Olympics were in Mexico City.

17 I heard Walter Cronkite oppose the Vietnam War on national TV.

18 I elected Richard Nixon president.

19 I saw Helen Keller die.

20 The U.S. fought in Vietnam in my time.

I am 1968.

2O QUESTIONS

INSTRUCT PLAYERS THAT "I AM A YEAR."

1 The Yankees won my World Series.
2 I witnessed the German economy collapse.
3 I first saw Al Jolson in *The Jazz Singer*.
4 I opened the Holland Tunnel in New York.
5 I saw Sacco and Vanzetti electrocuted.
6 Philo T. Farnsworth demonstrated the first all-electronic TV during me.
7 I saw Trotsky expelled from the Russian Communist Party.
8 I watched Greta Garbo in *Love*.
9 The U.S. population was 119,035,000 during my time.
10 Henri Cochet won my Wimbeldon.
11 I made Clara Bow an "It Girl."
12 I saw Davidson Black discover "Peking man."
13 I saw Socialists riot in Vienna.
14 Charlie Chaplain is one of my stars.
15 My favorite movie is *Wings*.
16 The Harlem Renaissance was thriving during me.
17 The sum of my digits is 19.
18 Calvin Coolidge is my U.S. president.
19 My last two digits add up to 9.
20 I helped the Roaring Twenties roar.

I am 1927.

2O Questions

INSTRUCT PLAYERS THAT "I AM A YEAR."

1 Britney Spears was the queen of pop during me.

2 Kurt Vonnegut did not die during me.

3 I watched Venus Williams win at Wimbeldon.

4 I saw Wisconsin defeat Stanford University in the Rose Bowl.

5 A lot of people said I had a problem.

6 I brought the Oxygen network to life.

7 I saw the Yankees win the World Series.

8 I heard America Online and Time Warner announce their merger.

9 Walter Matthau passed away during me.

10 My U.S. president was Bill Clinton.

11 I watched Regis Philbin host *Who Wants to be a Millionaire*.

12 Harry Potter's *Goblet of Fire* topped The New York Times Bestseller List during me.

13 Voters elected a dead man senator from Missouri during my time.

14 *Survivor* was my top TV show all summer.

15 I saw Elian Gonzales go home with his father.

16 I saw *Charlie's Angels* at the movies.

17 *Forbes* magazine placed Larry Ellison over Bill Gates as the richest man in the world during me.

18 The St. Louis Rams won my Super Bowl.

19 I saw the Olympics in Sydney, Australia.

20 I end in zero.

I am 2000.

2O Questions®

INSTRUCT PLAYERS THAT "I AM A YEAR."

1 Zip codes got started during my time.
2 I saw the Bears beat the Giants.
3 I saw Alcatraz prison close its doors . . . this time without anyone inside.
4 I witnessed the birth of Mike Myers. Yeah, baby.
5 I put the first woman in space.
6 I watched *The Beverly Hillbillies* on TV.
7 I saw Andy Warhol's *Soup Cans* at the Guggenheim Museum.
8 I saw the "hot line" installed between the White House and the Kremlin.
9 I heard Dr. Martin Luther King say "I have a dream."
10 I viewed the *Mona Lisa* in New York.
11 Lee Harvey Oswald was killed during my time.
12 I saw a great train robbery in Glasgow.
13 I said goodbye to Robert Frost.
14 Kenya acquired independence during me.
15 I saw the Yankees play the Dodgers in the World Series.
16 Alaska and Hawaii were already states when I got going.
17 *The Birds* landed in theaters during my time.
18 John F. Kennedy's assassination shocked the nation during me.
19 I saw Sidney Poitier win the Oscar® for Best Actor in a Leading Role.
20 I saw Pope John XXIII die.

I am 1963.

2O Questions

INSTRUCT PLAYERS THAT "I AM A YEAR."

1 Postal rates increased during my time.

2 I'm not odd.

3 The Yankees beat the Braves in my World Series.

4 I saw the first domestic U.S. jet airline passenger service.

5 Robert Penn Warren won my Pulitzer Prize for American Poetry.

6 Boris Pasternak declined my Nobel Prize.

7 I named David Niven Best Actor in a Leading Role at the Oscars®.

8 I saw Khrushchev make it to the top.

9 I witnessed the first undersea crossing of the North Pole.

10 I saw Arkansas protest integration.

11 I gave Stan the Man his 3,000th hit.

12 I brought Michael Jackson into the world.

13 The *$64,000 Question* was on TV during me.

14 I saw the Colts beat the Giants in sudden death for the NFL championship.

15 Elvis enlisted during my time.

16 I saw John XXIII become the Pope.

17 In my time, Elizabeth Taylor's third husband, Mike Todd, was killed in a plane crash.

18 Eisenhower was my president.

19 *The Bridge on the River Kwai* received many of my Oscars®.

20 The sum of my digits is 23.

I am 1958.

2O Questions

INSTRUCT PLAYERS THAT "I AM A YEAR."

1 New York passed the first seat belt law during me.

2 I saw Ray Kroc die.

3 I gave Michael Jackson a Grammy Award for "Thriller."

4 I watched the first movie rated PG-13.

5 Desmond Tutu was awarded a Nobel Peace Prize during my time.

6 I saw the film *Ghostbusters*.

7 I attended the Jackson Five's "Victory Tour."

8 My Summer Olympics were in L.A.

9 I saw *Amadeus* at the movies.

10 I first heard Bruce Springsteen sing "Born in the U.S.A."

11 The Democrats had their convention in San Francisco during my time.

12 I saw Marvin Gaye killed by his father.

13 I brought *Jeopardy!* back to primetime.

14 The Bears won my Super Bowl.

15 I heard the Grateful Dead tour to sold-out shows.

16 Donald Duck had a happy 50th birthday during my time.

17 Ronald Reagan was my president.

18 I am a leap year.

19 George Orwell wrote a book about me.

20 I named Peter Ueberroth commissioner of baseball.

I am 1984.

20 Questions

INSTRUCT PLAYERS THAT "I AM A YEAR."

1   I am a year in the 20th century.
2   I still didn't allow women to vote.
3   I saw the birth of John F. Kennedy.
4   I am before Prohibition.
5   I saw the first Pulitzer Prize awarded.
6   I saw Degas and Rodin die.
7   I saw the Progressive Era start to wind down.
8   I saw the Lusitania sink.
9   I brought jazz great Thelonious Monk into the world.
10 I saw the U.S. declare war on Germany.
11 The Pope I knew was Benedict XV.
12 I saw Charlie Chaplin's yearly salary reach $1 million.
13 Russia found me revolting.
14 I read Freud's *Introductory Lectures on Psychoanalysis*.
15 Buffalo Bill died during my time.
16 No one won at Wimbledon during my time.
17 I saw Woodrow Wilson inaugurated.
18 George M. Cohan wrote "Over There" during my time.
19 I put the Espionage Act on the books.
20 I saw King Constantine of Greece abdicate.

I am 1917.

2O Questions

INSTRUCT PLAYERS THAT "I AM A YEAR."

1 I saw Herman Goering sentenced to death.

2 I saw snow in Palm Springs, CA.

3 Unlike my predecessor, I'm known for peace.

4 I'm not an Olympic year.

5 I saw the Eagles win the NFL title.

6 I saw the first fully-electric computer.

7 I saw a peace conference of 21 nations held in Paris.

8 I saw Albania become independent.

9 I saw Italy become a republic.

10 I heard Churchill give his "Iron Curtain" speech.

11 Harry Truman was my president.

12 I saw Europe begin to rebuild.

13 I saw Juan Peron elected President of Argentina.

14 I said goodbye to Gertrude Stein.

15 The Yankees won my pennant.

16 I witnessed African miners go on strike.

17 I saw Ernie Lyons win the first Manx Grand Prix.

18 I saw Laurence Olivier star in *Henry V*.

19 I saw *Notorious* hit the box office.

20 The sum of my digits is 20.

I am 1946.

2⊙ Questions

INSTRUCT PLAYERS THAT "I AM A YEAR."

1 I saw Norman Rockwell die.

2 I saw *Animal House* at the movies.

3 I saw the Cowboys win it all.

4 I bore the first "test tube baby."

5 I read *The World According to Garp*.

6 I elected the first non-Italian Pope.

7 I saw the mandatory retirement age change from 65 to 70.

8 I saw Jim Jones and 900 followers commit suicide in Guyana.

9 Bill Graham presented "A Day on the Green" in Oakland, California during me.

10 *Saturday Night Fever* was at the movies during me.

11 I saw Israel and Egypt outline a peace plan at Camp David.

12 I saw the last classic Volkswagen Beetle roll off the German assembly lines.

13 I saw San Francisco's mayor, George Moscone, assassinated.

14 I premiered *Dallas* on TV.

15 I saw Ali defeat Spinks in boxing.

16 I saw the Bullets take the NBA title.

17 I saw *Superman* on the big screen.

18 I watched the Yankees beat the Dodgers at the World Series.

19 I saw *The Deer Hunter* at the movies.

20 Jimmy Carter was my president.

I am 1978.

2O Questions

INSTRUCT PLAYERS THAT "I AM A YEAR."

1 I saw Macauley Culkin in *Home Alone*.
2 I opened the first McDonalds® in Moscow.
3 I watched *Cheers* become the number one TV show.
4 Dr. Seuss's *Oh, The Places You'll Go* topped my bestseller lists.
5 I saw the movie industry create NC-17.
6 I said goodbye to Sammy Davis, Jr.
7 Haiti held its first democratic election during my time.
8 Pat Riley was the NBA Coach of the Year during me.
9 Boris Yeltsin became the President of the Russian Federation during me.
10 Madonna made "Vogue" a hit during me.
11 I saw Margaret Thatcher resign as Prime Minister of Great Britain.
12 I united East and West Germany.
13 I saw Julia Roberts become a *Pretty Woman*.
14 I wore down Noriega in Panama.
15 I saw *The Simpsons* get their own TV show.
16 I witnessed Nelson Mandela released from a South African prison.
17 *Dances with Wolves* received my Oscar® for Best Picture.
18 I watched underdog Buster Douglas KO Mike Tyson in the ring.
19 I saw Iraq invade Kuwait.
20 The sum of my digits is 19.

I am 1990.

2O Questions

INSTRUCT PLAYERS THAT "I AM A YEAR."

1   I saw Austria declare war on Serbia.

2   I saw the U.S. Congress set up the Federal Trade Commission.

3   I said goodbye to Richard Sears.

4   I didn't award a Nobel Prize.

5   My U.S. president was Woodrow Wilson.

6   I saw Cleveland, OH install the first red and green traffic light.

7   My first-class U.S. stamp was 2¢.

8   I saw Army win my NCAA Football Championship.

9   Old Rosebud won my Kentucky Derby.

10 I saw the U.S. Ludlow Massacre.

11 "The St. Louis Blues" was a popular song during my time.

12 I saw the Woolworth Building become the world's tallest.

13 I saw the Western Federation of Miners overthrown by socialist mine workers.

14 I saw Rene Thomas win the Indy 500.

15 I am 15 years prior to Black Friday.

16 I saw the birth of William Burroughs.

17 I watched Gandhi return to India.

18 I saw the opening of the Panama Canal.

19 I was the first to read Robert Frost's *North of Boston*.

20 I saw Boston win the World Series.

I am 1914.

2O Questions

INSTRUCT PLAYERS THAT "I AM A YEAR."

1 I said, "So long," to martial arts master Bruce Lee.
2 I saw Chile undergo a military coup.
3 Henry Kissinger and Le Duc Tho shared the Nobel Peace Prize in my time.
4 Native Americans occupied Wounded Knee during me.
5 I appointed Clarence Kelley director of the FBI.
6 I first saw the Sears Tower.
7 Secretariat won my Triple Crown.
8 I saw the Roe vs. Wade Supreme Court decision.
9 Vice President Agnew resigned during me.
10 I premiered Woody Allen's *Sleeper*.
11 I saw Egypt and Syria attack Israel.
12 Sonny and Cher had a comedy hour during my time.
13 I opened the Board of Options Exchange in Chicago.
14 I witnessed a cease-fire in Vietnam.
15 I am not an Olympic year.
16 I heard Nixon say "I am not a crook."
17 *The Sting* earned the Best Picture nod at my Academy Awards®.
18 I saw Gerald Ford become vice president.
19 I launched Skylab.
20 I watched *M*A*S*H* on TV.

I am 1973.

2O Questions

INSTRUCT PLAYERS THAT "I AM A YEAR."

1 I first saw Britain's Clean Air Act introduced.

2 I saw the start of transatlantic telephone cable service.

3 I am in the last half of my decade.

4 *Peyton Place* was a best-selling novel during my time.

5 I saw Grace Kelly marry Prince Ranier.

6 I first saw *My Fair Lady* in New York.

7 I saw rock and roll become popular.

8 I saw Japan admitted to the United Nations.

9 I heard Allen Ginsberg's "Howl."

10 I saw boxer Rocky Marciano retire.

11 I watched *The Ten Commandments*.

12 I witnessed the *Invasion of the Body Snatchers*.

13 I watched the Andrea Doria sink off Nantucket Island.

14 I witnessed the birth of Bob Moog in St. Louis, Missouri.

15 I saw Nasser elected Egypt's president.

16 I saw Ed Sullivan introduce Elvis.

17 I am a big year for Baby Boomers.

18 I hosted the seventh Winter Olympics.

19 I saw the death of painter Jackson Pollack.

20 I first heard Elvis Presley's hit "Hound Dog."

I am 1956.

2O Questions

INSTRUCT PLAYERS THAT "I AM A YEAR."

1 I hosted the first Earth Day.
2 I saw Joe Frazier win the heavyweight title.
3 I acquitted the Chicago Seven.
4 I saw the AMA support abortions for social and economic reasons.
5 I premiered the film *M*A*S*H*.
6 American women celebrated fifty years of suffrage during my time.
7 Allende became the president of Chile in my time.
8 I celebrated Beethoven's 200th birthday.
9 Anwar Sadat was elected president of Egypt in my time.
10 I banned cigarette ads on U.S. TV.
11 I saw the first U.S. postal strike.
12 Aleksander Solzhenitsyn won my Nobel Prize in Literature.
13 I laid rock legends Jimi Hendrix and Janis Joplin to rest.
14 I witnessed U.S. forces enter Cambodia.
15 I watched the Orioles defeat the Reds in the World Series.
16 I saw the establishment of the Environmental Protection Agency.
17 I saw Nixon in the White House.
18 George C. Scott refused my Best Actor Oscar® for *Patton*.
19 I watched *All My Children* make its television debut.
20 I saw the NFL and the AFL merge.

I am 1970.

2O Questions

INSTRUCT PLAYERS THAT "I AM A YEAR."

1 I saw actor and female impersonator Divine die in his sleep.

2 I watched *thirtysomething* on TV.

3 I saw Yellowstone National Park on fire.

4 *Big* was a hit at my box office.

5 I read Tom Wolfe's *Bonfire of the Vanities*.

6 *The Cosby Show* was one of my top-rated shows.

7 I introduced the world to *Rain Man*.

8 Debbie Gibson and Tiffany competed for my Debut Artist of the Year honors.

9 I saw the Lakers win the NBA title.

10 I called a truce in the Iran-Iraq war.

11 I saw Manuel Noreiga indicted for drug smuggling.

12 I gave George Bush a promotion.

13 I witnessed an earthquake in Armenia.

14 I caught Ben Johnson using steroids.

15 The Dodgers won my World Series.

16 I heard Mike Tyson and Robin Givens say "I do."

17 President Reagan visited the U.S.S.R. during me.

18 I watched Greg Louganis win gold.

19 I saw the Olympics in Korea.

20 I am a leap year.

I am 1988.

2O Questions

INSTRUCT PLAYERS THAT "I AM A YEAR."

1 I saw Xerox manufacture the Xerox 914, the first plain paper copier.

2 Linda Blair was born during my time.

3 I saw Wham-O's Hula Hoop® become a national rage.

4 I saw Navy beat Army 43-12.

5 I listened to Bobby Darin sing "Mack the Knife."

6 I saw Jaroslav Heyrovsky win the Nobel Prize.

7 I watched the unveiling of the hovercraft.

8 Barbie® made her debut appearance during my time.

9 The sum of my digits is 24.

10 I saw *Ben Hur* at the movies.

11 I saw Danny's Coffee Shops renamed Denny's.

12 I saw the Colts dominate the Giants in the NFL.

13 I saw Manhattan blacked out from a massive power failure.

14 I saw *Gypsy* on Broadway.

15 I saw Ingemar Johansson win the Heavyweight title.

16 Tennis star John McEnroe was born during my time.

17 I saw *Maverick* and *The Rifleman* on TV.

18 I welcomed Alaska as the 49th and largest state.

19 Hawaii became the 50th state during my time.

20 I am the year the music died.

I am 1959.

ABOUT THE AUTHOR

Always ahead of the game, Bob Moog's newest undertaking is truly novel. As a game inventor, his credits include such favorites as 20 Questions® and 30 Second Mysteries®. As the president of University Games, he has propelled the company he founded with his college pal into an international operation that now boasts five divisions and over 350 products. Whether hosting his radio show "Games People Play," advising MBA candidates or inventing games, Bob sees work as serious fun. He now brings his flair for fun and learning to the bookshelf with the Spinner Books line.

Enjoy Spinner Books?
Get an original game!

Find these games and more at
or your nearest toy store.